Esther

Every decision is from the LORD

First published 2008

ISBN No: ISBN: 978-1-905975-14-3

Published by Biblical Frameworks

Reg. Office: 23 Coe Lane, Tarleton, Preston, PR4 6HH.

Cover design, typesetting and production management by Verité CM Ltd, Worthing, West Sussex UK +44 (0) 1903 241975

Illustrations by Richard Thomas

Printed in England

Biblical Frameworks is registered in England No: 5712581
Charity No: 1116805.

Contents

'Who's directing this?'

1. Introductory thoughts from Paul Blackham

The longest chapter in the Bible is all about... the Bible! Psalm 119 is all about the wonder of the Word of God. Verse 103 shows us the heart of someone who really loved the Bible. He cries out to the LORD God:

Psalm 119:103 – "How sweet are your words to my taste, sweeter than honey to my mouth!"

Whether you are reading the Bible alone or in some kind of group with others, expect to be thrilled by the words of the Living God. This is not like reading any other book. When we read and study the Bible the ultimate Author can be present with us, showing us His words and applying them to us.

Thousands of small groups are starting up all over the world – but what is it that is going to sustain them? It has to be the Bible.

So often, people don't quite know what to do with these small groups. Meeting together, sharing testimonies and experiences or sharing the odd verse is ultimately too sparse a diet to sustain people's spiritual needs in the long run, and really help them to grow.

What is needed is confidence in the Bible, and the ability to go to a *book* of the Bible rather than just an isolated verse. Each book of the Bible was written with a purpose, and it is only as we digest it as a book that we understand the real message, purpose, direction, storyline and characters.

It's a lot easier than people often think. You might think, "Oh, I can't manage a whole book of the Bible", but what we're trying to do in Book by Book is to break it down and show that it's easy.

The Bible was written not for specialists, not for academics – it was written for the regular believers, down the ages.

The world is in desperate need for answers. How can the world live at peace? How can we live together with justice and truth and compassion? There are so many religions and so much division and bloodshed: what is the real and living way that takes us to the Living God who can give us all a new beginning?

The Bible is the answer of the Living God to all our questions.

Our desire is that many Christians would experience the joy and confidence in the Scriptures that is found throughout Psalm 119 – "How sweet are your words to my taste, sweeter than honey to my mouth!"

II. All about Book by Book

a. What is Book by Book?

Book by Book is a Bible Study resource with accompanying DVD. It has been designed principally for use in small groups, but can also be used for personal study or larger group situations.

b. The structure of Book by Book

The Study Guide

The Study Guide provides the following features for each section of study:

- A Key Truth to focus on the most important truth in that section of the Bible Book.
- A Mind-Map diagram giving an overview of the study.
- An explanation of the Bible text, divided under suitable headings.
- Further Questions, to stimulate deeper thought and discussion.
- A week of suggested daily Bible readings to fill out and explore the themes from the study.
- A Bible Study, with detailed questions, designed to lead the individual or group deeper into the text.
- A Bible Study answers section at the back of the study guide, for extra help if need be.

The DVD

Key features provided on each DVD are as follows:

- There is a 15 minute discussion on the DVD linked to each section of the Study Guide Bible passage
- The on-screen host is Richard Bewes, with co-host Paul Blackham. A specially invited guest joins them in the Bible discussions.

C. Some tips on how to use Book by Book

The beauty of Book by Book is that it offers not only great Biblical depth, but also flexibility of approach to study. Whether you are preparing to lead a small group, or study alone you will find many options open to you.

And it doesn't matter if you are a new Christian or more experienced at leading Bible studies, Book by Book can be adapted to your situation. You don't need to be a specially trained leader.

Group study: preparing

- Select your study (preferably in the order of the book!)
- Watch the DVD programmes
- Read the commentary
- Use the suggested Bible questions...
- ...or formulate your own questions (the mind maps and key truths are a great guide for question structure)

Group study: suggested session structure

We recommend you set aside about an hour for each study

- 5 minutes – read the relevant section of the Bible
- 15 minutes – Watch the DVD programme
- 30 minutes – work through the Bible study questions (either your own or the ones in the guide), allowing time for discussion
- 10 minutes – If the study got the group thinking about wider issues of life today, Then consider the Further Questions to stimulate a broader discussion
- aking it further – Suggest that group members look at some of the Daily Readings to follow up on the theme of the study

Given the volume of material you may even choose to take two weeks per study – using the DVD to generate discussion for one week and the Bible Study questions for the next.

Individual study

There is no set way to conduct personal study – here are some ideas:

- Select your study (preferably in the order of the book!)
- Read the Bible passage and related commentary.
- Try looking at the Mind-Map diagrams and seeing how the book has a structure.
- Take a look at the Key Truths and decide if they are the same conclusions you had reached when you read the book.
- Perhaps focus on the week of daily Bible reading to help you to explore the rest of the Bible's teaching on the themes of each section of study.
- Work through the Bible Questions. Don't worry if you get stuck, there is an 'answers' section at the back of the guide!

III. An introduction to Esther

The book of Esther might seem strange at first because the LORD God is not mentioned once in the whole book. Why would such a book be in the Bible at all? Has it got anything to tell us or is it just an interesting ancient story? We need have no fears. By the time we get to the end of the this book we will be full of praise and worship. The book of Esther will capture our hearts and minds for the Living God.

The very fact that the Living God is 'invisible' throughout this book is no accident. As we go throughout our day-to-day lives we do not 'see' the providential hand of our heavenly Father or the glorious rule of our ascended LORD Jesus or the comforting, strengthening care of the Holy Spirit. Nevertheless, as children of the Living God, we are always kept in His Almighty care. While we are in the challenges, trials and sufferings of life we rarely understand why the Father has allowed these things to happen to us. However, when we look back at our lives we so often praise the wonderful and gracious guidance and wisdom of the Father. The book of Esther teaches us that the Living God is hard at work in the complexities of our lives even though He rules from His throneroom in the *invisible* creation.

The Bible does not hide from the difficulties that women face in a sinful world in which sinful men tend to 'rule over' them (Genesis 3:16).

> The Bible pulls no punches about the fates of women: They are raped (Dinah in Genesis 34; Tamar in 2 Samuel 13), forced into marriage (the dancers at Shiloh in Judges 21, Esther in Esther 2), offered to other men by their fathers (Michal in 1 Samuel 18) or husbands (Sarah in Genesis 12 and 20), abandoned (Hagar in Genesis 16 and 21, Samson's wife in Judge 14), dismembered (the Levite's concubine in Judges 19)... They must fight for property (daughters of Zelophehad in Numbers 27). They must prove their worth by bearing sons (Leah and Rachel in Genesis 29-30). They must survive by their wits (Tamar in Genesis 38, Shiphrah and Puah in Exodus 1, Jael in Judges 4, Abigail in 1 Samuel 25, the wise women of 2 Samuel 14 and 20) and by their tenacity (Moses' mother in Exodus 2... Bathsheba in 1 Kings 1, the Shunamite

> woman in 2 Kings 4). Yet if the biblical world is a fairly unsafe place for women, it mirrors the experience of most women still. Women's freedom even in the first world remains tenuous, constricted by the fear of attack by strangers, employers, and husbands. In many parts of the third world, women's freedom hardly exists at all. That is why stories of courageous women still stand out disproportionately to their length in the biblical canon – because we still need them so very much. Stories of biblical women whose efforts are met by divine cooperation and community affirmation inspire hope for contemporary women...[1]

However, on another level this book teaches us about the safety of the Church in a world that can be very hostile. The book of Esther shows us how the LORD Jesus will always protect His Bride, the Church. Whoever is an enemy to His Bride is His enemy too, and will certainly come to a very nasty end. The Lord Jesus laid down His life for His Bride and is very jealous for her love and safety. The book of Esther should give deep assurance to us, as members of Christ's Bride, that no matter what threats come against us, no matter what persecution we have to face, yet He absolutely guarantees us a wonderful, glorious conclusion.

1 Patricia Tull: "Esther and Ruth" published by WJK London, 1998, pages 1-2

The Studies

'How is this going to end'

Study 1 The Abuse of Power

Esther chapter 1

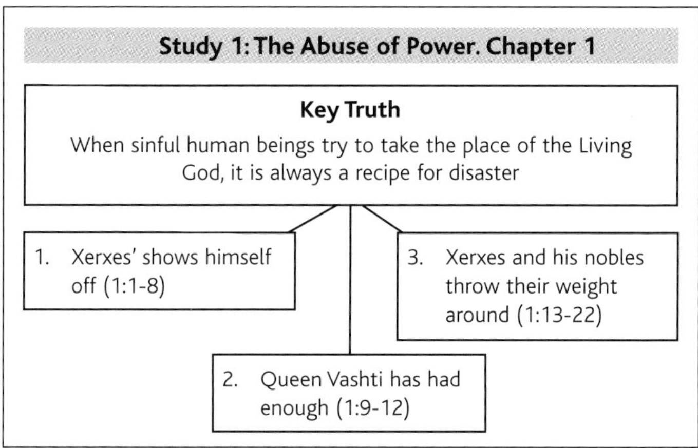

1. Xerxes' shows himself off (1:1-8)

The book of Esther begins with a massive demonstration of worldly power. We are taken to the heart of the Persian Empire, into the throne room of this mighty superpower.[2] In verse 1 we are shown Xerxes'[3] great empire stretching from India to Egypt. We are left with the impression that the affairs of this world lie in the hands of the politicians, that the world is shaped and governed by human power.

This book of the Bible will force us to think about this. Where do we think the world is ruled from? Is it ruled from the 'royal throne' in Susa (or London, Geneva, Moscow, Beijing, Rome, Baghdad, Washington, Nairobi

2 It is thought that Xerxes reigned from 485-465 BC. It is worth remembering that the events of the book of Daniel took place about 100 years earlier.

3 His name has several forms. because of the difficulty of capturing his name in different languages. His Greek form (Xerxes) is an attempt to express his Persian name Khshayarsha. The Hebrew form of this was probably pronounced something like achashverosh. This is why some English versions of the Bible have his name as Ahasuerus, following the Hebrew form rather than the Greek.

or Tokyo)? Or is the world ruled from the throne room of the Father where the Son sits enthroned? This question will confront us time after time throughout our lives, sometimes in very painful ways. Until we are at peace with the Bible's answer to the question we will always struggle to act and never know true contentment.

Xerxes celebrated the third year of his reign with a huge banquet. He gathered together all the leaders of his powerful empire so that they could bask in the glory of the Persian empire. Millions of people were governed and controlled by these officials and generals. Xerxes organised a 6 month exhibition of all the treasures of the empire. How incredible and intimidating this exhibition must have been to the many people who took the tour! Notice that the purpose of the exhibition in verse 4 was not to marvel at the achievements of the *empire* but "the splendour and glory" of *Xerxes'* majesty. This a clear sign of the problems that we will find in Xerxes.

Xerxes was not satisfied by the 6 month display of his 'splendour and glory'. Next he held a banquet lasting *seven* days. It seems likely that it was no accident that the banquet lasted *seven* days. The creation of the world took seven days and ever since then the world has divided up its time into this seven day pattern. A man like Xerxes would choose a seven day banquet in order to mirror the great work of creation. This is further confirmed by the fact that he held the banquet in his personal garden. The Garden of Eden is called the Garden of God in the Bible[4], so Xerxes holds his seven day celebration in the Garden of Xerxes for everybody in the capital Susa! Xerxes seems to position himself as (at the very least) the mirror of the Living God on earth.

The pride of Xerxes is also shown by the way he decorated his 'garden'. His blue and purple linen seems to echo the courtyard of the tabernacle of the LORD described in Exodus 38. The temple of Solomon in Jerusalem had been destroyed by the Babylonians about 150 years earlier, so there must have been records of the architecture and furnishings of the temple. His use of the pillars with silver rings also indicates this kind of knowledge and symbolism. He formed a pavement of precious metals and jewels (Esther 1:6). If we remember the banquet with God in Exodus 24:9-11 or the

4 Ezekiel 28:13; 31:8-9

throne room of heaven in Revelation 4:1-6 we get an insight into the way that Xerxes viewed himself. If we remember that the book of Daniel had been written 100 years before we can understand how Xerxes got so much knowledge of heavenly realities. A book of such literary and theological significance, written by such a high official in the empire, would certainly have been in the royal library. Daniel's work included a vision of the throne room of heaven (Daniel 7:9-14), so it is not too much to imagine that Xerxes saw himself as a Son of Man figure over all the nations.

Surrounded by his nobles, on his pavement of precious stones, in his enclosed garden, with officials from across the world coming before him to marvel at his 'glory', Xerxes had divine pretensions.

The special guests to Xerxes' banquet were pampered from his special wine cellar (verses 7-8). Every guest received individual treatment, according to their own individual preferences. The fact that Xerxes could deliver such incredible hospitality would have amazed the world.

It would be very hard not to be overwhelmed by King Xerxes after all this. If you were one of the Hebrew saints visiting this display of human glory you would probably feel a bit shaken. The loud message ringing in your ears would be that Xerxes was the ruler of the world, that all the nations lived under his power and provision. You would be living in a superpower empire far greater than little Israel had been, witnessing the glory of the nations paraded before your eyes. What would you think? What would your prayer time have been like that evening when you got back home? What Scriptures would you have read to give you a sense of perspective?

The same challenge faces us today. The wheels of international power may often seem far removed from the gospel that we live by. Many of us around the world are confronted by the glory and splendour of human politics and rulers. Even Christians can become deceived by this and think that real power lies in the hands of men like Xerxes.

2. Queen Vashti has had enough (1:9-12)

Xerxes' wife, Queen Vashti, held a more modest banquet for the women in the royal palace (verse 9). The fact that we are told nothing about this banquet helps us to see the distribution of power and pride in the royal household. Our suspicions are confirmed as the story unfolds.

The name 'vashti' is Persian for 'beautiful woman', which may have been imposed on her by Xerxes, because she is nothing to him other than a kind of trophy supermodel.

On the seventh day of his banquet, Xerxes summons his bride. On the seventh day of creation the LORD God entered into His rest (Genesis 2:2-3). The whole creation now waits to return to that rest, which was lost in the rebellion of Adam & Eve. This is why the seventh day has a symbolism throughout the Bible connected to the hope of the new creation and the marriage feast of the Lamb. If we are right in seeing the theological symbolism in Xerxes' behaviour then it happens here too. On the seventh day of Xerxes' feast he called for his bride... however his behaviour to his bride fell very far short of the way that the Divine Son of Man treats His Bride, the Church.

In verse 10, we see that Xerxes had too much to drink. This is bad for anyone, but particularly bad in a king who wields so much power.

> Proverbs 20:1 "Wine is a mocker and beer a brawler; whoever is led astray by them is not wise."
>
> Proverbs 23:29-35 "Who has woe? Who has sorrow? Who has strife? Who has complaints? Who has needless bruises? Who has bloodshot eyes? Those who linger over wine, who go to sample bowls of mixed wine. Do not gaze at wine when it is red, when it sparkles in the cup, when it goes down smoothly! In the end it bites like a snake and poisons like a viper. Your eyes will see strange sights and your mind imagine confusing things. You will be like one sleeping on the high seas, lying on top of the rigging. "They hit me," you will say, "but I'm not hurt! They beat me, but I don't feel it! When will I wake up so I can find another drink?"

Xerxes had been hanging out with 'the boys' and he had certainly lost his wisdom and his mind imagined confusing things. In verse 11 he made a terrible mistake. As the husband of Vashti it was his duty to lay down his life for her.

> Ephesians 5:25-33 "Husbands, love your wives, just as Christ loved the church and gave himself up for her to make her holy, cleansing her by the washing with water through the word, and

> to present her to himself as a radiant church, without stain or wrinkle or any other blemish, but holy and blameless. In this same way, husbands ought to love their wives as their own bodies. He who loves his wife loves himself. After all, no-one ever hated his own body, but he feeds and cares for it, just as Christ does the church – for we are members of his body. 'For this reason a man will leave his father and mother and be united to his wife, and the two will become one flesh.' This is a profound mystery—but I am talking about Christ and the church. However, each one of you also must love his wife as he loves himself, and the wife must respect her husband."

Xerxes may have seen himself as the Son of Man over all the nations, but he most certainly did not imitate the selfless, self-sacrifice of the Son of Man. The top priority of any husband is to do everything he can to care for his wife, to protect her, to help her to be holy and perfect.

Xerxes behaved like a drunken yob.[5] He sent seven of his mutilated assistants to bring his wife to be paraded in front of the crowds. It is disgraceful behaviour. For Xerxes, Vashti is just an object to be paraded. When we consider the way that women are so displayed in modern life, whether in magazines or on the internet, we see that Xerxes view of women has come back with renewed vigour.

Thankfully Vashti had had enough. She must have been completely fed up with Xerxes parading the 'splendour and glory of his majesty' for the last six months. This must have been the final insult that pushed her over the edge. She simply refused to comply with Xerxes outrageous demand (verse 12).

Full of alcohol, inflated with his own importance, surrounded by fawning followers, Xerxes could not comprehend that somebody had dared to defy his will. We see just how little love he had for his wife by his reaction in the following verses.

3. Xerxes and his nobles throw their weight around (1:3-22)

Full of his rage and indignation, Xerxes called together the so-called wise men who were his best buddies (verses 13-14). When Xerxes puts his

5 The Hebrew word for the banquet would literally mean 'drinking party'.

loaded question to his 'advisors' (verse 15) they, of course, give him just the kind of answer that he wanted. Far from giving him wise marriage advice, they pander to his pride and rage.

Imagine Xerxes going to real marriage counsellors.

Marriage counsellor: "I see that you have had some marriage difficulties."

Vashti: "Well..."

Xerxes (interrupting): "Yes.. you see she won't do exactly what I say as soon as I say it no matter how unreasonable my demands."

Marriage counsellor (after a shocked silence): "I think we will need more than one session here."

Well, Xerxes didn't speak to genuinely wise counsellors, but rather to these nobles who were only interested in saying exactly what he wanted to hear. Memucan was the spokesman of the group and provided quite a speech (verses 16-20).

He began by portraying Vashti's behaviour as an offence against the entire Persian empire! If he wanted someone to keep the matter in perspective then he could not have picked anyone worse than Memucan. The fear that Memucan articulates is that other women in the empire might just follow Vashti's example and also refuse similarly unreasonable demands made by their husbands (verse 18). Of course, if that really happened it could only be good news for the Persian Empire, but that was not how 'wise' Memucan saw it. In fact he predicted that allowing wives to have any independence would lead to "no end of disrespect and discord".

Therefore Memucan's conclusion was that 'if it pleases the king' (verse 19... which it, of course would!), he should publicly divorce Vashti and make sure everybody everywhere heard about it (verse 20). Apparently this would keep all the Persian wives in order![6]

It is no surprise that the king and his nobles thought this was a great idea. In their drunken stupor such self-serving advice must have made a lot of sense. Verse 22 is the awful conclusion to a grim chapter of the Bible:

6 We could note the strangeness of Memucan's solution: Vashti is to be banned from being in the place she refused to go, the presence of Xerxes!

(Xerxes) sent dispatches to all parts of the kingdom, to each province in its own script and to each people in its own language, proclaiming in each people's tongue that every man should be ruler over his own household.

Xerxes went to a lot of trouble to make sure all the different nations and language groups in his empire heard what he had to say – "every man should be ruler over his own household."

In this pagan world, in rebellion against the Divine Messiah, the relationship between a husband and wife becomes a very ungodly situation. Instead of a husband's self-sacrificial love and care and a wife's freely given respect, we have instead almost the direct opposite. Xerxes' view of marriage is a minature version of his own megalomanic rule over his empire.

Praise God that the church of Jesus Christ has brought the revolution of Jesus to marriage and the dignity of women. When we see how Jesus dealt with women in the gospels we see what the real ruler of the nations thinks about women. Jesus gave up all He had, even enduring the agony of the Cross, in order to put the interests and well-being and dignity of His Bride first. In doing that He set the standard for marriage in every age. In the Hebrew Scriptures the whole book of Hosea teaches the same truth. When we read the first chapters of Hosea and we see the terrible heartbreak and abuse that the prophet endures for his wife, we are amazed to see that it is the way that the LORD God perseveres in love for His wife, the Church.

It must be our prayer that we can repent of ever following the ways of Xerxes, and that instead we would always conform our marriages to the pattern of Christ and His Church.

Study 1 Bible Questions

Esther 1:1-12

1. Verse 1. What would it feel like to live under a massive world empire that spanned two continents? What was the size of Israel compared to an empire that stretched from Africa deep into Asia?
2. Verses 2-3. Imagine the different nations and languages present at the banquet. What did this say about King Xerxes?
3. Verse 4. Why did he need to display 'the glory of his majesty' for 6 months?
4. Verses 5-6. Consider Xerxes' enclosed garden. Consider the pavement of precious stones and the free access that all the people had to this palace and garden. Compare this to Exodus 24:10 and Revelation 21:15-27. What is Xerxes trying to say about himself?
5. Verses 7-8. Xerxes seemed to have all the different wines from all the different countries and regions, with a bewildering range of wine goblets. How did this reveal his empire and majesty?
6. Verse 9. Why did Vashti's banquet get such a brief mention? What does this tell us about life in Xerxes' empire?
7. Verses 10-12. Consider Proverbs 31:1-5. How does Xerxes compare to the wisdom of Proverbs?
8. How can we be faithful to Jesus under the great world empires of this age? What are the great empires that span the continents? How should we pray to the real King?

1; Duter. Chp 1 – How a King should behave.

Eph Chp 5 – Husbands duty

Study 1 Further Questions

1. Multinational companies seem to wield more power than nations. In what ways are our lives shaped and influenced by these massive world-spanning companies? How does their advertising influence us? How do they affect our attitude to money, possessions and life-style?
2. How could a Jesus-community live in order to withstand the seductions of the world-empires of this age? How can we be free from materialism or a lust for power?
3. Is it ever right for us to spend lots of money on our own house and garden? Is this storing up treasure on earth?

Study 1	Daily Readings
Day 1	Esther 1:1-12
Day 2	Esther 1:13-22
Day 3	Exodus 24:1-18
Day 4	Isaiah 2:1-22
Day 5	Isaiah 6:1-13
Day 6	Revelation 18:1-24
Day 7	Revelation 19:1-21

The daily Bible readings are an opportunity not only to read through all of the material in the book under study, but also to read parts of the Bible that relate to the themes and issues that we have been considering. We try to make sure that we receive light from the whole Bible as we think through the key issues each week.

Study 2 Esther – Married to Power

Esther Chapter 2

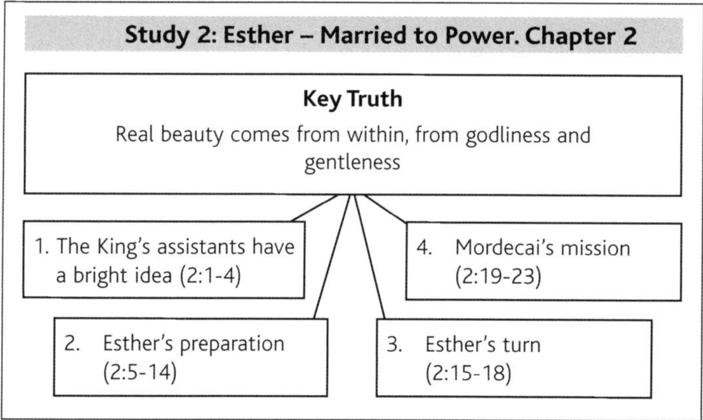

1. The King's assistants have a bright idea (2:1-4)

Chapter 2 begins with Xerxes missing his beautiful wife. It is the morning after the night before, so to speak. He has sobered up and realises that he has just lost his wonderful wife. Chapter 1:19 makes it very clear that Xerxes cannot undo the drunken madness that he had done. His so-called 'wise' law cannot be changed.

His assistants know that Xerxes is pleased so long as he gets exactly what he wants, so they come up with just the kind of bright idea that would appeal to him. They suggest that it might be good to use the powers of the empire to collect together all the most beautiful girls from all the nations and regions under the control of Xerxes... then Xerxes could try out each one of them for a night... and then he could pick one of them to replace Vashti. A special building and a staff could be allocated for the process (verse 3) and beauty treatments for up to one year could be given to these girls to maximise their beauty (verse 12). After their night with Xerxes they would be imprisoned in another building (verse 14) so that they could never know natural human marriage, hoarded up as trophies for Xerxes.

This idea is so ghastly, so debased, so demonic that in any decent company these assistants would have been severely punished for even thinking such foul thoughts. Only the darkest and most selfish instincts of sinful flesh would entertain such a fantasy. However, Xerxes (verse 4) thought it was a good idea and went along with the 'advice'. This is a man who is used to indulging his sinful flesh.

Why does Xerxes bother with the pretence of having 'advisers' when all they ever do is tell him what he most wants to hear? That is also part of our sinful human nature. In the New Testament Paul warned Timothy about how hard it is to tell people the truth when they really only want to hear a comfortable lie.

> 2 Timothy 4:3 "Instead, to suit their own desires, they will gather around them a great number of teachers to say what their itching ears want to hear."

Human nature was no different in Esther's day as Timothy's... and it is no different today. All too often the clever arguments and the slick presentation cover up sordid desires and selfish agendas. The book of Esther has pulled back the curtain of the highest level of political decision making and shown us that however this was 'sold' or 'spun' to the empire it was ultimately a sinful man indulging his evil desires.

> "What pains were taken to humour the king! As if his power and wealth were given him for no other end than that he might have all the delights of the sense wound up to the height of pleasurableness, and exquisitely refined, though at the best they are but dross and dregs in comparison with divine and spiritual pleasures." (Matthew Henry, commenting on this passage).[7]

The play-boy mentality, the 'lad' culture, promises fulfilment, thrills and pleasure, yet what seeds are sown that must be reaped? What costs are attached, what victims are created, what damage is done?

7 "...analogies to modern beauty pageants, though tempting, are quite misleading, since admission is involuntary and the king controls the losers as well as the winner. A closer contemporary analogy is the kidnapping of girls and women, lured into sexual slavery in foreign countries by false promises of respectable employment." (Tull, page 11).

> "While the benefits of seeking the king's pleasure have so far been taken for granted by the men, women seem to need guidance understanding their place. The one woman most expected to set an example of queenly pliability simply refused to play the game. Recognizing her act as powerful and potentially influential, royal officials have twice legislated worldwide womanly compliance: first, by ordering all the married women to obey their husbands, and second, by rounding up the unmarried for the king's pleasure. Though the narration keeps a light touch, we should not forget the disruption and even violence implied in such actions. All is not right in the world of King Ahasuerus." [8]

King Xerxes ruled much of the world, but in every sinful human heart the same desire festers, to assert our own will, to get our own way, to have things as we want, even if it just means being left alone. The pleasures we seek when we try to be on the throne are always tainted.

The wonderful, healthy, enriching pleasures of the creation – friendship, marriage, worship, food, fellowship, music, industry, Sabbath – all these are ours when we follow the way of Jesus, and have no sting in the tail.

2. Esther's preparation (2:5-14)

It all looks very bad indeed when we see Esther carried away by the imperial soldiers to be one of the many raped by Xerxes (verse 8). Mordecai had cared for Esther because she was an orphan. Her original Hebrew name was Hadassah, which means 'myrtle', but her Persian name meant 'star' – which is what the LORD God determined her to be in the Persian Empire. [9]

Mordecai was her uncle and clearly cared for her as if she were his own daughter (verse 7). In verses 5-6 we are informed that Mordecai was a member of that ancient church, Israel, and that he had not forgotten that they were in exile, away from the Promised Land and Jerusalem. His grandfather, Kish, had been one of those taken into exile under

8 Tull, page 13

9 Myrtle is a family of trees and shrubs that are usually evergreen. Myrtle plants often produce aromatic oils and are used in spices (e.g cloves). In the Bible the myrtle seems to indicate fertility and usefulness – see Isa. 41:19; 55:13; Zech. 1:8, 10f.

Nebuchadnezzer. For more than 50 years the people of Israel had been free to return to the Promised Land to rebuild the nation. A man called Mordecai is mentioned in Ezra 2:2 as going to help with the rebuilding work. It is certainly possible that it was the same man when he was young, but that when the building of the temple stopped he felt that he could do more good watching out for the LORD's people in Persia.

Can we imagine that pain in Mordecai's heart when Xerxes' soldiers came to take Esther away? He had cared for her, brought her up, protected her... but now he was unable to protect her from such mighty human power. Perhaps he tried to hide her, but she was so beautiful (verse 7) that he would never have been able to do that for long. His name means 'bitter', and it would not be surprising if that is how he felt at this time.

Esther and Mordecai must have felt so powerless and helpless at that time.[10] It seemed that their lives lay in the hands of human rulers and human power. What hope had they got against such power and organisation? Esther's hopes and dreams for the future were snatched away from her. If she had dreamt of marrying a godly man who would love her and lay down his life for her, now she faced a life of being raped by the king and then locked away for the rest of her life. What a grim prospect!

If Esther and Mordecai had thought about the providence of their Heavenly Father at this time it would have seemed very dark and mysterious to them. If they thought in the way that most of us do, then they would have wondered "Why didn't the Most High care for them? How could He allow this sort of thing to happen? Surely this kind of thing could not be under His control?"

The book of Esther wants us to think about this. In chapter 2 of Esther it looks as if Xerxes and his empire have the first and last word over the world. Will it look like that when we get to the end of the book?

Maybe many of the girls couldn't handle the situation, but Esther seemed to get on with it and made a good impression on Hegai, who was in charge of the preparation process (verse 9). Hegai picked her out for

10 All of the initial verbs linked to Esther are passive: she was brought up, adopted and taken. She is told how to act, even in the life of the harem. She is *acted upon*. It is all meant to make us realise just how vulnerable she is before the unyielding power of the empire.

special treatment and she even got her own team of beauty experts in the best facilities in the harem.

Mordecai cared so much for Esther (verses 10-11) that he basically spent all his time hanging around outside the harem, hoping for information about her, wanting her to know that he was praying for her and thinking about her.

Mordecai had given her an odd instruction (verse 10): to keep quiet about her nationality and family background. Was she to be a 'secret believer' in the hostile environment of the Persian court? Did he realise that she did not yet have the spiritual maturity to be an isolated witness in Xerxes' harem? Was he simply asking her to be silent about her ethnicity but ready to speak about her faith? Did Mordecai sense that it was not the right time in the Father's providence for Esther to reveal her identity? All of these questions have been posed by Christians about Esther down the generations and it is not easy to know exactly why Mordecai asked her to behave in the way that he did.

If we compare her to Daniel we can perhaps get a better understanding. Daniel and his friends were in a position where they could get on with obeying the Law of the LORD, and when they were questioned about this they explained why they behaved in the way that they did. Esther's situation was harder and messier. She was being forcibly married to a *pagan* man. The Law forbids this (Deuteronomy 7:3-4). It is reasonable to assume that Esther does not start with the spiritual maturity that we find in Daniel because it seems a very big step when she comes to her 'Daniel moment' in chapters 6-7. Esther is caught up in a messy, compromised situation and might have had a lot of spiritual maturing to do in that situation before she could handle the intense hostility of a man like Haman. Perhaps we should see that Mordecai wanted Esther to 'be wise as a serpent and as harmless as a dove' (Matthew 10:16). Esther had to be patient in the very difficult situation that faced her. She had to trust in her Heavenly Father to watch over her, just as her earthly guardian Mordecai watched over her.

(Mordecai) did not bid her deny her country, nor tell a lie to conceal her parentage; if he had told her to do so, she must not have done it. But he

only told her not to *proclaim* her country. All truths are not to be spoken at all times, though an untruth is not to be spoken at any time. She being born in Shushan, and her parents being dead, all took her to be of Persian extraction, and she was not bound to undeceive them.[11]

In verse 12 Esther undergoes the year long beauty treatment. For the first 6 months she was simply bathed in oil of myrrh. In the Bible, myrrh is used for the preparation of the body – either for love (Psalm 45:8; Proverbs 7:17; Song 1:13; 3:6; 4:6, 14; 5:1, 5, 13) or for burial (Matthew 2:11; John 19:39). After this 6 month period of intense body preparation, her cosmetics regime was developed for the next 6 months. In this time her beauty team would 'do her colours', prepare her hair, lipstick, nails, makeup etc.

Even today we find people planning their weddings more than 18 months in advance in order to get all their preparations in place. Several wedding advisory services talk about a beauty regime lasting for over a year in the run up to the wedding.

The Bible has a wonderful balance in all this. There are plenty of examples of celebrating physical beauty. The lovers in the Song of Songs fully appreciate each other's physical charms. It was the LORD God who made us with such beautiful, wonderful, fascinating attractive features. He designed us to be so appealing to each other, and there is nothing *godly* about trying to hide or reject or be ashamed of our physical beauty.

So, on the one hand it is wrong when people disdain physical beauty as somehow 'unspiritual'. That kind of attitude has nothing to do with the Bible's perspective on the glories of the human body. On the other hand, the Bible strongly warns us against thinking of beauty as *merely skin deep*. If we invest *only* in the superficial aspects of beauty we will miss the truly deep and captivating beauty that comes from the inner aspects of the person. The apostle Peter has the balanced view:

> 1 Peter 3:3-5 "Your beauty should not come from outward adornment, such as braided hair and the wearing of gold jewellery and fine clothes. Instead, it should be that of your inner self, the

11 Matthew Henry

> unfading beauty of a gentle and quiet spirit, which is of great worth in God's sight. For *this* is the way the holy women of the past who put their hope in God used to make themselves beautiful."

Beauty must not *rest* on our outward presentation. Rather it should rest on 'the *unfading* beauty of a gentle and quiet spirit'. Peter adds the wonderful comment in 1 Peter 3:5 that this was the beauty regime of the holy women of the past – for their whole lives rather than just one year. This is such a relevant comment because Sarah was still so attractive when she was older. For example, when she was 65 she was so beautiful that Abram feared for his life when they went to Egypt:

> Genesis 12:11-16 "As he was about to enter Egypt, he said to his wife Sarai, "I know what a beautiful woman you are. When the Egyptians see you, they will say, `This is his wife.' Then they will kill me but will let you live. Say you are my sister, so that I will be treated well for your sake and my life will be spared because of you." When Abram came to Egypt, the Egyptians saw that she was a very beautiful woman. And when Pharaoh's officials saw her, they praised her to Pharaoh, and she was taken into his palace. He treated Abram well for her sake, and Abram acquired sheep and cattle, male and female donkeys, menservants and maidservants, and camels."

Abraham caused a lot of trouble for Pharaoh with his lies, but Sarah must have been very beautiful to have attracted the attention of the ruler of Egypt. Peter explains that Sarah made herself so beautiful because she put her effort into her inner beauty rather than the more insubstantial beauty of outward appearance.

So, going back to Xerxes, we again see the problems in his worldview. We saw in his attitude to Vashti that he had no understanding of real marriage and human sexuality. For him, Vashti was a beautiful object to show off and use. The moment that she showed that she was a real person who would not tolerate that kind of relationship, Xerxes divorced her! In his world-wide search for a new wife, his criteria for finding a new queen are so inadequate and selfish. How could his process of selection hope to find the suitable personal qualities for the queen of a mighty empire?

Once again we see that the situation seems to be completely cut off from the kingdom of the Living God. Once again it all looks as if the shallow power of human sin is in charge.

3. Esther's turn (2:15-18)

Eventually Esther gets to the front of the queue and has to spend the night with Xerxes. Esther had put herself completely in the hands of Hegai and taken his advice about the whole process. We are told this so that we realize that Esther was much more than a beautiful body. She was wise and gracious. She won the favour of everybody she met (verse 15)... even Xerxes (verse 17). The king chooses Esther as his new wife and crowns her queen of the Persian Empire.

Snatched from her normal life, Esther found herself at the very centre of Persian power (insofar as a woman had any power in Xerxes' empire!). We are never told what Esther thought about all that happened to her. Everyone knew what had happened to Vashti, so did Esther fear that she would be also caught in such problems? Did everyone know what a difficult character Xerxes was in private? Perhaps Esther had been praying that a woman would have been chosen as the new queen before her turn had come so that she might have been allowed to return to her own life. Had Esther's night with Xerxes been a dreadful heartbreak as her own hopes and dreams had finally been destroyed... or had Esther given herself up to the new situation during the year of preparation?

Esther's own state of mind is difficult to determine, but it must have been a bewildering experience. Another worldwide celebration was held with an imperial holiday. Another one of Xerxes' banquets was arranged, with all the rulers and civil service, in order to honour Esther as the new Persian queen. We can be sure that the very best of the empire's facilities were put at her disposal.

Esther must have often wondered to herself 'why is this happening to me?'

4. Mordecai's mission (2:19-23)

In verse 19 we see that Mordecai was still watching over Esther. Now that Esther was queen he surely knew that his prayers and support were even more important. Esther continued to do just what Mordecai told her to do (verse 20). Again we are told that she had kept her family background hidden, because the whole story will turn on this key fact.

The virgins were gathered a second time (verse 19). It is difficult to know what this means. It might have meant that the rest of the virgins were assembled for the celebration, before being released to return home, or it might refer to them being assembled around Esther at her coronation. Whatever the case, Mordecai was still there, still caring for Esther, still keeping in contact with her, offering her whatever advice that he could.

Notice that now Mordecai was "sitting at the king's gate" (verse 19 & 21). Throughout the Bible the gate is the place of public government and judgement (see Genesis 23:10-20; 34:20-24; Deut 21:19; 22:15; 25:7; Ruth 4:11; Job 29:7; Lam 5:14). This may well mean that Mordecai had been appointed as a judge or government official, possibly as a result of Esther's coronation. If that is so it is another example of the Heavenly Father's wonderful care, making sure that Mordecai would be able to stay close to Esther even in the royal palace.

Mordecai's place at the city gate gave him access to what was happening around Xerxes and Esther, and in that position he was able to be a great help to Xerxes as well as Esther. The city gate was the place were wisdom was given and discussed.

Proverbs 24:7-8 "Wisdom is too high for a fool; in the assembly at the gate he has nothing to say."

At the city gate Mordecai's wisdom is revealed and he is able to uncover an evil plot to kill Xerxes. From what we have seen of the king it is not hard to imagine that he had made many, many enemies – the fiancés of the virgins stolen from across the empire; the people who had been part of Vashti's circle of influence; people who had also displeased the whims of the king during one of his drinking parties.

The two officers in charge of the gate where Mordecai was sitting hatched a plot to assassinate Xerxes. When Mordecai found out about this he got a message to Esther to warn the king. In spite of all the heartbreak that Xerxes had caused Mordecai, nevertheless Mordecai was a good citizen and a godly man.

Esther told Xerxes what was going on and made sure that full credit was given to Mordecai for uncovering the assassination plot.

The two men were killed on the gallows. The Hebrew for 'hanged on a gallows' here would more accurately be rendered 'hanged on a tree' (as the King James version has it). This is important because to be hanged on a tree is, in the Bible, the cursed death. To be hanged on a tree in death is to be under the curse of the Living God. The relevance of this will be seen by the time we get to the end of the book.

Mordecai's mission of uncovering the assassination plot was properly recorded in the king's official records. This seems such a small detail at this point, but the book of Esther is teaching us that all of life, down to the tiniest details, lies in the hands of the Glorious Father who sits enthroned in heaven with His Eternal Anointed Son and Holy Spirit.

Where is the real throne of power – Susa or heaven?

Study 2 Bible Questions

Esther 2:8-17

1. Verse 8. Think about the nouns ('order'; 'edict') and verbs ('bought'; 'put under'; 'taken to'; 'entrusted to'; 'charge of') used in this verse. How do they show the way all these women were treated?
2. Verse 9. How does the experience of Esther compare with the experience of Daniel and his companions in Daniel chapter 1?
3. Verse 10-11. Were Mordecai and Esther right to keep her nationality a secret? Is it ever right to be a 'secret believer in Jesus'? How might we be like Mordecai in supporting a 'secret believer'?
4. Verse 12. How should Christians deal with beauty treatments? In Song of Songs beauty products are seen in a positive way. In 2 Samuel 12:20 David uses lotions to improve his appearance. What is the right balance for women and men?
5. Verses 13-14. What more do we learn about the kind of man Xerxes was?
6. Verses 15-16. What can we learn about the kind of woman Esther was?
7. Verse 17. What might Esther have thought about all that happened to her? How could she have handled all this as a Christian believer?

Study 2 Further Questions

1. Thousands and thousands of women and children are trafficked for sex today. How can this happen on such a large scale? What kind of society allows so much slavery to happen? Can there be a new William Wilberforce who will ban modern slavery?
2. Viewing pornography is not a victimless sin. Thousands of women are coerced and exploited to produce this material. How is this abuse of women tackled in your church?
3. How can the community of Jesus show a better way in terms of 'The Beauty Myth'? Do we just go along with the myth? How can we encourage every person to be full of gratitude for the gracious gift of their wonderful body?
4. What do you think about the Dove campaign for real beauty? www.campaignforrealbeauty.com

Study 2 Daily Readings

Day 1	Esther 2:1-14
Day 2	Esther 2:15-23
Day 3	Ephesians 5:1-20
Day 4	Ephesians 5:21-33
Day 5	1 Peter 3:1-7
Day 6	Daniel 1:1-7
Day 7	Daniel 1:8-21

The daily Bible readings are an opportunity not only to read through all of the material in the book under study, but also to read parts of the Bible that relate to the themes and issues that we have been considering. We try to make sure that we receive light from the whole Bible as we think through the key issues each week.

'God versus the devil'

Study 3 Haman – Corrupted by Power

Esther chapter 3

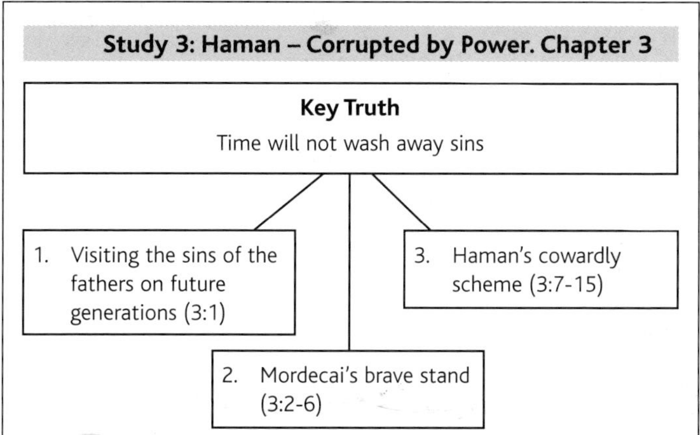

1. Visiting the sins of the fathers on future generations (3:1)

Chapter 3 begins in a very strange way. If we set out these verses without the chapter and verse divisions see how it reads:

Mordecai found out about the plot and told Queen Esther, who in turn reported it to the king, giving credit to Mordecai. And when the report was investigated and found to be true, the two officials were hanged on a gallows. All this was recorded in the book of the annals in the presence of the king. *After these events*, King Xerxes honoured *Haman* son of Hammedatha, the Agagite, elevating him and giving him a seat of honour higher than that of all the other nobles.

We are expecting Mordecai to be honoured for his outstanding service to Xerxes... but instead another man, an Agagite, was honoured.

We are supposed to gasp in horror when we realise that Haman was an Agagite... and if we know our Bibles well enough that is just what we do.

This takes us back many hundreds of years to the time when the church was delivered from slavery in Egypt. The Amalekite people saw the Hebrews and decided to kill the weak and elderly who were straggling behind the main body of the people. It was an act of such hard-hearted evil that the LORD God passed righteous judgement on them.

> Deuteronomy 25:17-19 "Remember what the Amalekites did to you along the way when you came out of Egypt. When you were weary and worn out, they met you on your journey and cut off all who were lagging behind; *they had no fear of God*. When the LORD your God gives you rest from all the enemies around you in the land he is giving you to possess as an inheritance, *you shall blot out the memory of Amalek from under heaven. Do not forget!"*

The Israelites forgot. When they took possession of the Promised Land they did not bring the LORD's judgement against the Amalekites. However, some 400 years later, when Saul was made king, the LORD sent Samuel to *remind* Israel of this work of judgement that still had to be carried out. The Amalekites were a people who had no fear of God and it was more urgent than ever for the LORD's judgement to fall on them.

> 1 Samuel 15:1-11 "Samuel said to Saul, "I am the one the LORD sent to anoint you king over his people Israel; so listen now to the message from the LORD. This is what the LORD Almighty says: `I will punish the Amalekites for what they did to Israel when they waylaid them as they came up from Egypt. Now go, attack the Amalekites and *totally destroy everything that belongs to them. Do not spare them; put to death men and women, children and infants, cattle and sheep, camels and donkeys.'"* So Saul summoned the men and mustered them at Telaim – two hundred thousand foot soldiers and ten thousand men from Judah... Then Saul attacked the Amalekites all the way from Havilah to Shur, to the east of Egypt. He took Agag king of the Amalekites alive, and all his people he totally destroyed with the sword. *But Saul and the army spared Agag* and the best of the sheep and cattle, the fat calves and lambs – everything that was good. These they were unwilling to destroy completely, but everything that was despised and weak they totally destroyed. Then the word of the LORD came to Samuel: "I am grieved that I have

> made Saul king, because he has turned away from me and has not carried out my instructions."

Saul allowed Agag, the king of the Amalekites to live, which deeply grieved the LORD. Just as the earlier Israelites, Saul thought that it wasn't necessary to kill absolutely all of these people. Samuel challenged him about this and killed Agag himself (1 Samuel 15:32-33), but it seems that Saul's disobedience had allowed some members of Agag's family to escape. When we are reading that part of 1 Samuel we might forget about that disobedience. Surely it won't matter? Perhaps the LORD's judgements were too harsh and didn't need to be so ruthlessly carried out.

So, when we get to Esther 3:1 we are supposed to gasp in horror as we realise that not only did Agag's family survive, but one of his descendants has just walked onto the centre-stage of the Persian empire, taking the honour that belonged to Mordecai.

The lesson here is very clear. If we disobey the LORD God, it might look as if there are no consequences at first... but we cannot disobey the Father, Son and Holy Spirit with impunity. Sin is more dangerous than we ever imagine. It can never be contained or controlled. So often modern readers of Joshua think that the LORD was too harsh in his judgements against the deeply entrenched wickedness of the Canaanite people. However, the story of Esther vindicates the judgements of our LORD. Shall not the judge of the entire world do what is right?

2. Mordecai's brave stand (3:2-6)

If we did not know all about the background history of Haman the Agagite we might have found Mordecai's actions a little odd. Xerxes had commanded that all the government officials acknowledge the authority and honour of Haman... but Mordecai refused.

This caused quite a stir in the civil service. Why would a man like Mordecai, who had actually saved the life of Xerxes, now refuse to obey such a minor command of the king? It requires explanation. If Mordecai wants to keep his own family background secret then he cannot really explain his behaviour to them. The civil servants keep pestering Mordecai about this, and he did explain to them that he was a Jew (verse 4), but he did not seem to provide any further information. So, eventually the matter has to be reported to Haman.

3. Haman's cowardly scheme (3:7-15)

Initially Haman was simply very angry with Mordecai (verse 5), but when he learned that Mordecai was a Jew Haman realised that he had an opportunity to take it all to a much deeper level. The people of the LORD God had destroyed his nation long ago, leaving only a few of them to keep the memory of the Amalekites going. Now he had a chance to strike back at these people and their LORD God. Haman set himself the task of destroying all the Jews, wiping the church off the face of the earth.

Now the book of Esther takes a turn so much darker even than what we have read so far. The story is lifted beyond the troubles of a few individuals into the realm of the fate of the entire world. If the Church of the Living God were destroyed then there could be no hope for the world. The whole world would have no escape from the total destruction that must come on the Day of God.

Verse 7 is one of the key verses in the whole book. Haman got his men together to cast the lot (the *pur*) to find out when was the best month to have all the Jews killed. They did this in the first month, but the lot *just happened* to fall for the twelfth month, giving almost a year for things to happen.

It is vital that we remember this when we get to the end of the book of Esther. The book ends with a feast celebrating the fact that the LORD God controls the casting of lots.

> Proverbs 16:33 "The lot is cast into the lap, but its every decision is from the LORD."

Haman must have thought that his own wretched god/gods had guided him, so he went to talk to Xerxes. Mordecai, a Jew, had just shown exceptional faithfulness to Xerxes, and yet Haman paints a picture of Jews being a dangerous, rebellious ethnic group within the empire who refused to obey the king's laws. Haman presents the matter almost as if he *had* uncovered a plot to overthrow the empire, and he even offers his own money to fund the extermination of this civic threat (verse 9).

Xerxes is not a man for careful detail in his government, so he does not investigate the accusations that Haman made. He simply handed over his signet ring of authority, refused Haman's money and allowed him to carry out whatever he thought was necessary.

Can we imagine the gleeful satisfaction on Haman's face when his plan seemed to go so smoothly? He would finally be able to take revenge against the LORD God and His people.

Again the wheels of civic power are set in motion across the huge empire (verse 12). Haman wrote his orders in every language using the king's name and signet ring. Haman wanted to make sure that nothing could go wrong.

> Esther 3:13-14 "Dispatches were sent by couriers to all the king's provinces with *the order to destroy, kill and annihilate all the Jews – young and old, women and little children – on a single day*, the thirteenth day of the twelfth month, the month of Adar, and to plunder their goods. A copy of the text of the edict was to be issued as law in every province and made known to the people of every nationality so that they would be ready for that day."

Notice the redundant ferocity of the order. How is it possible to not only destroy, but also kill and annihilate all the Jews? Haman has some deep issues in his heart and mind. Notice also that he extends the order to cover 'young and old, women and little children'... just as the LORD God had done against the Amalekites hundreds of years before. Haman knew his history.

The chapter ends with a wonderful little sentence: "The king and Haman sat down to drink, but the city of Susa was bewildered'. Xerxes and Haman had just ordered the murder of a huge number of people... so they decided to get drunk. It is staggering that men of such low character were in such places of power, but that is also what the book of Esther is showing to us. Human power may seem so mighty and deep, and yet it is so often founded and wielded by such flawed and fractured people.

> Proverbs 31:4-5 "It is not for kings, O Lemuel – not for kings to drink wine, not for rulers to crave beer, lest they drink and forget what the law decrees, and deprive all the oppressed of their rights."

The people of Susa were *bewildered* by all this. They probably were thinking, 'what do they get up to in that royal palace? Why do all these people need to be killed? They have done nothing wrong?' It is as if we are carried outside the fantasy world of Xerxes and Haman and allowed to glimpse how strange it all seemed to the regular citizens of the Persian Empire.

This chapter might leave us also feeling bewildered. History seemed to be turning in a very unfortunate direction and it looked as if extremely bad times lay ahead for the church of the Living God.

Agagite -

Proverbs 16 v33.

Study 3 Bible Questions

Esther 3:1-11

1. Verse 1. Why are we told that Haman was an Agagite? What would the elevation of Haman have meant to the ancient church? Why would the Living God allow such a thing to happen?
2. Verse 2. Mordecai had told Esther to remain as a secret believer. Why does he stand out so much from the crowd? Why couldn't he just go along with the crowd towards Haman?
3. Verses 3-4. Mordecai was breaking the law. Was this acceptable? Acts 5:29. When can we do this? What laws could we break in our country today?
4. Verses 5-6. Why does Haman react in such an extreme way? Is this more than just the pride of Haman?
5. Verse 7. The date was set randomly, by lot. What was significant about the outcome? How does this show us the hand of the Living God at work?
6. Verse 8. What do we learn about the ancient church from Haman's speech?
7. Verses 9-11. How can the lot be under the LORD's control, but Haman seem to be so out of control?

Study 3 Further Questions

1. Mordecai refuses to bow down to Haman. When do we have to make a stand and when do we keep quiet? What are the issues that should drive us to make a public protest? When should we take to the streets to demonstrate? Should Christians ever do that?
2. If someone in our office or neighbourhood ridicules or attacks the church, how should we deal with the situation? How do we bless the ones that persecute us? Can we bless a person by confronting them and challenging their attitudes?
3. Is anything ever 'random'?

Study 3	Daily Readings
Day 1	Esther 3:1-6
Day 2	Esther 3:7-15
Day 3	Daniel 3:1-15
Day 4	Daniel 3:16-30
Day 5	Psalm 56
Day 6	Psalm 59
Day 7	Revelation 13:1-18

The daily Bible readings are an opportunity not only to read through all of the material in the book under study, but also to read parts of the Bible that relate to the themes and issues that we have been considering. We try to make sure that we receive light from the whole Bible as we think through the key issues each week.

Study 4 Mordecai – Using the Power

Esther chapters 4-6

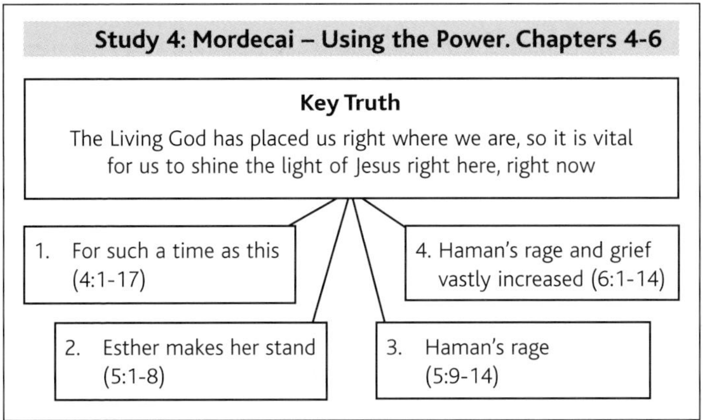

1. For such a time as this (4:1-17)

If Mordecai had ever had any intuition that there were difficult times ahead for the Jews[12], then when he heard of this edict he knew that the day had come. Mordecai did not immediately throw himself into political intrigue, trying to find a way of getting around the king's order. Mordecai knew that there was no hope for them now... other than the true King over all kings seated on the throne of heaven.

---

12 The Septuagint (Greek translation) version of Esther has a kind of prologue at the beginning that introduces us to Mordecai. He is described as a government official, but most importantly he had a vision in the second year of Xerxes reign warning him that there would soon be a clash between two enemies, that the righteous people would be prepared for death, but that the light would dawn and they would be saved. If there is any truth in this then it would certainly explain why Mordecai wanted Esther to keep quiet about her family background. He would have known in advance that a time of great crisis for the Jews was coming and he would have wanted Esther to keep a low profile until the right time.

Mordecai tore his clothes, put on sackcloth and ashes and wept bitterly.[13] Because the book of Esther is deliberately silent about the Living God, there is no explicit reference to Mordecai *praying*, but when we look at other people in the Bible who also tore their clothes and used sackcloth and ashes, we get a good idea of what Mordecai must have done.

The first thing to note is that the use of sackcloth and ashes is a sign of repentance from sin.[14] We might think that Mordecai has nothing to repent of, but when we understand the mind of the Hebrew saints we will see that they viewed life much more holistically than perhaps many of us do. They lived under the blessings and curses of the Law of Moses and they knew that if the Church was threatened with disaster it could only be because the LORD was bringing the curses of the Law against them. They knew that the first order of business was *repentance* when the judgements of the LORD God came upon the people of Israel.

It is very interesting to read the prayer of Daniel when he also tore his clothes and put on sackcloth and ashes when faced with disaster against Israel in exile:

> Daniel 9:3-19 "I turned to the Lord God and pleaded with him in prayer and petition, in fasting, and in *sackcloth and ashes*. I prayed to the LORD my God and confessed: 'O Lord, the great and awesome God, who keeps his covenant of love with all who love him and obey his commands, *we have sinned and done wrong*... Lord, you are righteous, but this day we are covered with shame – the men of Judah and people of Jerusalem and all Israel, both near and far, in all the countries where you have scattered us because of our unfaithfulness to you... The Lord our God is merciful and forgiving, even though we have rebelled against him; we have not obeyed the LORD our God or kept the laws he gave us through his servants the prophets... Just as it is written in the Law of Moses, all this disaster has come upon us, yet we have not sought the favour of the LORD our God by turning from

13 Does Mordecai weep so loudly and bitterly because it was his own actions that had brought about Haman's attack on the Jewish people? If Mordecai had compromised about his identity then Haman's fury against the Jews may not have arisen at this time. The Bible does not really lead us to think of Mordecai's grief as a self-pitying grief. Certainly his speech and actions have greater depth than that.

14 See Matthew 11:21; Luke 10:13

> our sins and giving attention to your truth. *The LORD did not hesitate to bring the disaster upon us, for the LORD our God is righteous in everything he does; yet we have not obeyed him.* Now, O Lord our God, who brought your people out of Egypt with a mighty hand and who made for yourself a name that endures to this day, we have sinned, we have done wrong. O Lord, in keeping with all your righteous acts, turn away your anger and your wrath from Jerusalem, your city, your holy hill. Our sins and the iniquities of our fathers have made Jerusalem and your people an object of scorn to all those around us... *We do not make requests of you because we are righteous, but because of your great mercy.* O Lord, listen! O Lord, forgive! O Lord, hear and act! For your sake, O my God, do not delay, because your city and your people bear your Name."

It seems quite right to assume that Mordecai prayed just as Daniel did. Mordecai knew that unless the Father had mercy upon His Church, they would certainly be destroyed. Mordecai is a wonderful example for us.

For myself, my first instinct in times of crisis is so often to think of things that I can do to deal with it. Mordecai's first instinct is to throw himself in repentance before the Living God.

It is *not* that Mordecai does nothing. We will see throughout this chapter that he does just the right things, but the *first* thing that he does is appeal to the true King.

Mordecai was not alone in his repentance. In verse 3 we read that the Jews across the whole empire had just the same reaction to the edict. They too began fasting, weeping and wailing – "many lay in sackcloth and ashes".

Haman's universal decree had not been published within queen Esther's chambers, because she had no idea what was troubling Mordecai so badly. Perhaps she had heard his wailing, and his dress would certainly have appeared very strange among the officials of the royal court! The clothing that Mordecai wears is an important theme in the book from this point. Esther tries to get him to put on different clothes, but he won't touch them (verse 4). So Esther orders Hathach to investigate the matter (verse 5).

When Hathach finds Mordecai, he is told the whole matter, down to the smallest details. Specifically Mordecai asks Esther to go to Xerxes to ask for mercy for *her* people. In telling Hathach that the people condemned are *Esther's* people, Mordecai clearly feels that the time for anonymity was over. It is time for Esther to use her position for the sake of the Church of the Living God. Hathach takes a copy of the edict back, reporting all that Mordecai had said.

Esther seems concerned by Mordecai's request. She does not refuse to do what Mordecai asked, but she makes Hathach go and explain the difficulties of such an action.[15] Xerxes was a very difficult man to deal with, even for his wife. He was not known for having much affection or romance for his wives. In fact (verse 10), Xerxes was so touchy and self-important that he had a law that if anybody even tried to speak to him without him first summoning them, they would be put to death! So severe was this law that the king had to have a special way of mercy: if a person had dared to speak to him, they could be spared only if he held out his golden sceptre.

Esther was particularly nervous because it had been a full month with no contact with her husband (verse 11). After all the trouble Xerxes had gone to find this wife it must have seemed strange that he didn't want to enjoy her company as much as possible... or perhaps he had had enough of beautiful young women for the time.

When Mordecai heard this answer from Esther he knew that it was time to give her the tough challenge that she needed. He had protected her before, even advising her to keep quiet about her spiritual identity, but it was time for her to grow up fast.

First, Mordecai tells her the hard facts (verse 13). Esther is a member of the Church and cannot escape the fate of the Church. Just because she lived within the palace she would not be spared. The law was absolute and universal in its scope. Her identity had already been revealed to Hathach so it wouldn't be long before others knew, including Haman.

15 People often assume that she was refusing to do what Mordecai asked, but it is important to notice that she did not do that. Esther has greater depths than anyone realizes – certainly more than either Haman or Xerxes realises.

Second, Mordecai shows a wonderful confidence in the providential care of the Father. He has absolute trust that even if some of the Jews are killed in the coming crisis yet some kind of deliverance would arise for them so that they would survive into the future. So Mordecai warns Esther that both the two of them would certainly not escape, living as they did under Haman's nose, but there certainly would be deliverance for some of the Jews from somewhere.

How can Mordecai be so utterly confident that the Church would not be annihilated? What divine promise supports this certainty?

> ...crucial to the background of the book of Esther is *the conflict described in God's words to the serpent, the devil's instrument*, in Genesis 3:15: "And I will put enmity between you and the woman, and between your offspring and hers; He will crush your head and you will strike His heel." Satan's activity is traceable throughout the Bible. His tracks may be discerned, together with the aliases he employs – in this case, that of Haman. Satan, the enemy of souls, was endeavouring to destroy the Jews, the people through whose seed the Messiah was to be born into the world, in order to make null and void God's promise of a Redeemer... God was committed to preserving the Jewish people so that from them salvation might go out into the ends of the earth... God's protection of his people was the protection of the Offspring of the woman though which he preserved and carried on his plan of redemption.[16]

As a godly man of faith, Mordecai trusted in the Promised Seed, the Coming Messiah, who had been prophesied since the world began. Think of the great prophesies of Moses, David and Isaiah concerning the Messiah – the Divine King, the Suffering Servant, the Seed of Abraham. Mordecai must have known the Scriptures and knew that no matter what plans Satan tried to bring about, no matter what murder and mayhem he caused, yet it was a divine certainty that somehow the seed of Abraham would survive so that The Seed of Abraham could be born to pave the way to the New Creation for people across the whole world.

16 Derek Prime: "Unspoken Lessons about the Unseen God" (Evangelical Press, Darlington, 2001) page 20-21

Third, many people see the end of 4:14 as the key statement for book of Esther: *"who knows but that you have come to royal position for such a time as this?"* We know that this book is teaching us that no matter how the decisions and 'chances' of life seem to go, yet we can be sure that everything is held in the care and direction of the Father, Son and Holy Spirit. We could answer Mordecai's question for him: our Heavenly Father knew that Esther had come to royal position for such a time. We have seen how His deep plans have been unfolding and He has made sure all the key decisions were exactly what He wanted them to be. Esther had been placed in exactly the place that God the Father wanted her to be, so that the plans of Haman could be thwarted.

Esther responds well to Mordecai's challenge. It is a wonderful moment in her personal development when she takes charge of the situation in verses 15-17. We have seen how *passive* Esther has been – everything has been done *to her*, whether for good by Mordecai or for ill by Xerxes and his agents. Now, however, she responds to Mordecai's words and she grasps the situation actively on her own terms. She *commands* Mordecai with forceful verbs: go; gather; do not eat or drink.

First, Mordecai is to gather the Church in Susa together. She knows that she needs the prayer and support of her spiritual family if she is to do what she must with Xerxes.

Second, she commands the Church family to go on a particularly severe fast for *three days* – no water as well as no food.[17]

Third, Esther and her staff will go on the fast as well. It is a great sign of her humility that even in her place of great privilege and honour, yet she is prepared to humble herself in the repentance and prayer along with the other believers.[18]

Fourth, Esther sets her purpose very clearly before her. She will go to the king *without being summoned*, even though it is a capital offence. "If I perish, I perish". It is thrilling to see such bravery and commitment from

17 Many of us will be familiar with the significance of 'three days' in the Bible. The fact that she indicates a three day fast shows that she is expecting an excellent outcome at the end of the fast.

18 It is fascinating that Esther's maids also go on the fast. Is this because she has witnessed to them and they have now become members of Israel too?

this young woman when the hour of decision was upon her. The real character and depth of Esther begins to be revealed. In all that has happened to her she has been prepared, not just in her outward form through the beauty treatments, but in her inner beauty and godliness through the trials she has faced in fellowship with Mordecai.

It would do well for all of us to pause and ask ourselves this same question. Why has God allowed *me* to live at this particular hour? To do what is right may mean that we must jeopardize our lives. Then we must face the issue and answer with this young queen, 'and if I perish, I perish'. Queen Esther answers the challenge of Mordecai. She who had been placed in the palace on flowery beds of ease had not succumbed to the luxury of her surroundings. She chose a course at terrible danger to herself for the sake of her oppressed people, the Jews. There is one thing to do always. Do what is right and leave the rest to God. God prepares people for emergencies. Failure is not sin: faithlessness is.[19]

I have often wondered if I could be so courageous in similar circumstances. Would I be ready to stand together with my church family under such severe persecution? When I examine my own heart I find only weakness, fear and compromise there, even though I feel it would be my greatest desire to be completely faithful to Jesus. So my prayer has become that Jesus would *make* me ready *when I need to be*, that He would prepare me for such a time. I know that in my own strength I can and will fail... but under the hands of our wonderful and wise and almighty Father, we can do the works that He has prepared in advance for us to do.

> Ephesians 2:10 "For we are God's workmanship, created in Christ Jesus to do good works, which God prepared in advance for us to do."

2. Esther makes her stand (5:1-8)

When the fast was completed Esther put on her best clothes and went to wait for an audience with her husband, the king. All her fears were immediately dispelled, because Xerxes was thrilled to see her and he held out his golden sceptre (5:2).

19 Henrietta Mears, "What the Bible is all about"

John Preston (1587-1628) produced a book called "The Golden Sceptre held forth to the Humble." The title is derived from this scene in Esther. Preston powerfully describes our Heavenly Father as a Great King into whose presence we cannot safely go. In fact, it is fatal for any sinner to be in the presence of the Living God. However, Preston portrays the gospel as the golden sceptre that is held out to the sinner to give them safe welcome into the presence of the Living God. This book is a classic collection of Puritan sermons. Nevertheless, it does feel a little bit strange to use Xerxes as a pattern of our Father in heaven!

Xerxes was so pleased to see Esther that he offers her half the kingdom if she asks for it! We have seen Xerxes getting drunk enough already to wonder at this point if he perhaps has had too much.

Esther's request is much more reasonable. She simple asks him (with Haman) to come to a special banquet that she had prepared for him. Given how much Xerxes likes banquets, this was a request that he was extremely happy to grant.

Verse 5 is one of the most delightful verses in the Bible.

> Esther 5:5 "Bring Haman at once," the king said, "so that we may do what Esther asks."

The joy of this verse is seeing it in stark contrast to what happened in chapter 1.

> (Xerxes) calls for Haman saying, 'Bring Haman quickly, *so that we may do as Esther desires*' (5:5). Literally the Hebrew says, '*so we may do the word of Esther*'. This is a deliciously ironic twist on a king who only three chapters before was terrified that women might not do the word of their husbands. Vashti was banished for not coming when the king called, but now Esther has gotten away with coming when the king did not call. The king who worried about women obeying their husbands is now obeying his wife, and ordering Haman to obey her as well. And to add irony to irony, Haman not only obeys a woman, but delights in being hosted by a Jew – a Jew passing as a Persian so splendidly that she puts a lie to all he said about her people's disruptiveness.[20]

20 Tull, page 26

It is surely no surprise to us to see that (verse 6) the king and Haman got down to drinking wine quite quickly. In such spirits Xerxes once again makes his extremely grand offer of giving her half the kingdom if she only asks.[21]

Esther knew what she was doing. In 2:15 we were told that Esther won the favour of everyone she met, and here we begin to see why. She was a woman of great wisdom and care. She wanted to peak the interest of the king, charm him, delight him with her company, win his affection for her. He had enjoyed the banquet so how pleasing it must have been for him to learn that he was being invited to *another* one the following night. She specifically invited Haman, once again.

3. Haman's rage (5:9-14)

One of the most satisfying aspects of this section of the book of Esther is following the emotional roller-coaster that is Haman. In 5:9 "Haman went out that day happy and in high spirits". He already enjoyed the honour of king Xerxes, but now it seemed that was also being admitted into the unimaginably privileged state of dining with the king and queen in their private banquet.

> Verse 12 – "I'm the only person Queen Esther invited to accompany the king to the banquet she gave."

We can imagine him grinning and hugging himself in sheer self-congratulatory joy. Not only had he arranged for his ancient enemies, the LORD's people, to be annihilated, but his own personal standing was fantastically high.

However, it all comes crashing down by the time we get to the end of the verse: "But when he saw Mordecai at the king's gate and observed that he neither rose *nor showed any fear* in his presence, he was filled with rage against Mordecai."

We can imagine that Haman was planning on capping his wonderful evening by strolling past his hated enemy Mordecai, who he felt sure would have been quivering in fear waiting for the terrible day of genocide to arrive. However, Mordecai feared the LORD God and therefore did not fear Haman at all.

21 Compare the foolish and wicked king Herod making the same offer in Mark 6:21-27.

Proverbs 29:25-26 "Fear of man will prove to be a snare, but whoever trusts in the LORD is kept safe. Many seek an audience with a ruler, but it is from the LORD that man gets justice."

Haman trusted in the human ruler, Xerxes – and was an emotional wreck. Mordecai trusted in the LORD and was confident that one way or another justice would be done. In spite of all the benefits that Haman had, he could not enjoy them as long as that one lowly Jewish man was sitting nearby (verse 13).

If Xerxes had advisors, so did Haman (verse 14). Verse 11 captures a strange scene, as Haman forces his friends and family to listen as he relates to them just how wonderful and honoured a man he really is. When he finally gets to the thing that concerns him, they recommend him to build a 75 foot wooden structure[22] for Mordecai to be hanged on.[23] They knew that nothing would cheer Haman so much as this thought – "This suggestion *delighted* Haman, and he had" the 'tree' set up.

Mordecai should be (impaled), not just high enough to do the job but eight stories high, so that everyone in the city can see... Since Mordecai will not rise *up* to bow *down*, and Mordecai's actions *lower* Haman's *high* spirits, Mordecai must be strung *up* fifty cubits high, and that will *raise* Haman's spirits.[24]

4. Haman's rage and grief vastly increased (6:1-14)

The king had a sleepless night – too much wine, excitement, rich food or worry could all have been contributing factors. Thankfully, he knew the perfect remedy for insomnia – history books! So he ordered a member of his personal staff to read some history out loud for him.

However, he became wide awake as the story of Mordecai uncovering the assassination plot was read out. It was quite possible that Xerxes may

22 Note that the NIV use of the word 'gallow' is a little misleading. It is more likely to be a stake for impalement than a gallows for a rope hanging. The Hebrew word *ates* simply means tree. It would probably clearest, in terms of understanding the Bible's view of such things, for us to simply say that Haman set up a 75 foot *tree* for Mordecai to be killed on.

23 In chapter 6:13 we learn that his advisors knew that Mordecai was a Jew and that it is impossible to stand against them. Why didn't they think to mention this when they were advising Haman in chapter 5?

24 Tull, 30

have been 'in high spirits' when Mordecai had performed his faithful service because the king didn't seem to have any recollection of how Mordecai had been rewarded for his valuable work. The assistants check the documents and report that nothing was done to reward Mordecai.

Xerxes owed his life to a man who had been completely ignored. We have come to realise that the king is not a man for careful, patient, measured action, so we are not surprised to see that he wants to do something about it immediately. Haman had come to secure the execution of Mordecai. He was too impatient to wait until the twelfth month. However, the providential care of our Father had foreseen all this. Just moments before Mordecai was to be sent to the 75 foot stake, the Father had arranged for Mordecai to be on the king's mind for very different reasons. Haman wanted to elevate Mordecai on a wooden stake ('tree'); the king wanted to *elevate* Mordecai in honour.

Xerxes summons Haman in to get his advice: "what should be done for the man the king delights to honour?"

It is one of the great moments in world literature. Haman hears the question as a subtle way of asking how the king may honour Haman (verse 6), so he really piles on the extravagant ways in which such a man could be honoured.

Notice Haman's repetition of the king's phrase – "the man the king delights to honour". We can imagine him quivering with pleasure each time he said it. The kind of honour that Haman describes is quite strange. A more practical man would have asked for something quite useful: a sum of money; a house; a grant of land. Haman has all of those things, so he asks for an excessively flattering *show* of personal honour.

- Bring a royal robe that the king has personally worn.
- Bring a horse that the king has personally ridden on.
- Make sure that the horse has a royal crest on its head.
- Entrust the horse and robe to a most noble prince.
- Make sure that this noble prince dresses the man to be honoured.
- The noble prince should lead the man on the horse through the streets.

The noble prince should proclaim the man's royal honour.

King Xerxes thinks it is a splendid idea – "Go at once..." (verse 10). Every time we read verse 10 we can't stop smiling. Can we imagine Haman's face when the king said "do *just as YOU have suggested* for Mordecai *the Jew*... Do not neglect anything you have recommended." Haman has designed a way of excessively honouring a man – and now *he* must carry it all out for Mordecai. Haman is the 'noble prince' in the description, not 'the man the king delights to honour'.

An important biblical theme, very much related to Haman's highs and lows, is the theme of reversal, of divine justice turning power upside down. This theme is so pervasive in the Bible, and so commonplace in Christian discourse, that its radical implications can sometimes be forgotten. Explicit reversals characterize many Proverbs, such as 16:18: 'Pride goes before destruction, and a haughty spirit before a fall.' Reversals also permeate narratives, such as the story of Joseph and his brothers (Gen. 37-50), the exodus of the Israelites from Egypt (Exodus 1-15), and the poem of Isaiah's suffering servant who will be exalted (Isa. 52:13-53:12). The narrative of reversal best known to Christians, of course, is the story of Jesus' death and resurrection.[25]

Throughout the book of Esther we are being taught to trust in the providence and justice of the Father, Son and Holy Spirit. At the moment we might see the enemies of Christ enjoying great success and honour, but we can be absolutely sure that justice will finally be done. Sooner or later, it is a divine certainty that the Church will be exalted and her enemies will be cast down.

Haman, who hates Mordecai so deeply, is forced to walk through the streets proclaiming how much the king honours Mordecai. When it was done he rushes home to get some comfort from his 'support network' (verse 12-13). However, they tell him what he least wants to hear. Not only did they think that Haman was on his way down, but that anyone is doomed to destruction that stands against the Church – "you will surely come to ruin!" The lesson that the Amalekites had to learn so long before was still being driven home to Haman.

Psalm 121:4 "He who watches over Israel will neither slumber nor sleep."

25 Tull, 30-31

Study 4 Bible Questions

Esther 4:1-14

1. Verse 1. Why does Mordecai put on sackcloth and ashes? In the Bible, what does this mean?
2. Verse 2. Why didn't the king allow sackcloth and ashes in his presence?
3. Verse 3. What do we learn about the ancient church from this behaviour? Could we imagine something like this happening today... even in just one country? What might create such a show of unity and prayer?
4. Verses 4-5. Why doesn't Esther understand what is going on?
5. Verses 6-8. Mordecai sends Hathak with a lot of information. Note three different pieces of information and instruction. Why did Mordecai tell Esther these three things?
6. Verses 9-11. What was it like to live in the court of Xerxes? What would it mean for Esther to do as Mordecai instructed?
7. Verse 12-13. Why did Mordecai tell Esther this harsh truth?
8. Verse 14a. What do we learn about Mordecai's trust in the real King, the LORD God?
9. Verse 14b. Why is this such an important question in the book of Esther? Is it fair to say that it is a summary of the whole book?

Study 4 Further Questions

1. We tend to think that our situation in life is not very promising. We tend to think that if we were somewhere else, in a different job, in a different church, we would be able to make more of a difference. When we read Mordecai's question in 4:14, how can we take a very different view of our place in life? Is it ever right to think the grass is greener in another field?
2. In chapter 5 we see Esther being as wise as a serpent and as harmless as a dove. Do Christians need to be wiser in the way we deal with 'the world'? How could we improve the world's perception of us? What are the dangers in doing this?
3. The book of Esther tells us so much about the dangers of power. How can Christians deal with these dangers?

Study 4 Daily Readings

Day 1	Esther 4:1-17
Day 2	Esther 5:1-14
Day 3	Esther 6:1-14
Day 4	Psalm 52
Day 5	Psalm 53
Day 6	Proverbs 25:1-28
Day 7	Luke 20:20-26

The daily Bible readings are an opportunity not only to read through all of the material in the book under study, but also to read parts of the Bible that relate to the themes and issues that we have been considering. We try to make sure that we receive light from the whole Bible as we think through the key issues each week.

Study 5 Some Justice through Power

Esther chapters 7-8

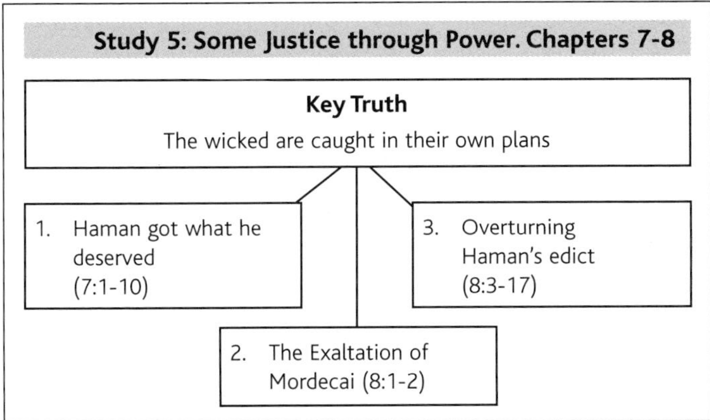

1. Haman got what he deserved (7:1-10)

What was Haman's state of mind when he arrived at the second of Esther's banquets? What a turn around since the last banquet ended!

In verse 1 the Hebrew literally is: "The king and Haman went to *drink wine with* Queen Esther." We can be sure that Haman was eager to fortify his fragile emotions with some alcohol.

The king, even after a full day to rethink what he had said, continued with the same offer to Esther: "Queen Esther, what is your petition? It will be given you. What is your request? Even up to half the kingdom, it will be granted."

Finally Esther answers the question, at the third time of asking (verses 3-5). Here we really appreciate how brilliant Esther was. The king probably expected her to ask for some great privilege or possession, and yet all she asks for is her life. "Grant me my life – this is my petition" (verse 3). Having won the king's affection so well, Esther makes the best possible use of her influence. Verse 4 is particularly skilful. She treats the king as if he were so high, so important, so engaged in matters of colossal significance, that if Esther and her people were simply going to be sold into slavery then she would not have dared to trouble him... but because they were all going to die, she dared to intrude upon his royal consciousness with her request!

It may not be very clear in most English translations, but verse 4 begins with Esther quoting Haman's edict word for word. Again, how wonderful it would have been to have seen Haman's face when he realised what was happening! His drink of wine had perhaps just begun to steady him from the trauma of honouring Mordecai, but now his world was really collapsing in a much bigger way. His advisory group had been proved right within hours of predicting his downfall.

In verse 5 Xerxes splutters out his outraged questions: "Who is he? Where is the man who has dared to do such a thing?"

Verse 6 is another moment that would look so good in the film version of this book. Esther turns and dramatically points her finger at Haman – "The adversary and enemy is this vile Haman."

Notice that Esther has positioned herself with the king over against Haman – "Haman was terrified before the king and queen."

The king is overcome with anger. It is as if he does not know what to do because his anger and shock is so great. He had placed so much trust and confidence in Haman, but he was more attracted to Esther than any other woman (2:17). If it is true that the fastest way to a man's heart is through his stomach, then Esther's two banquets had wooed the heart of the king to her even more. Xerxes goes out into the palace garden to digest the situation. He had to choose between two people who were very close to him. In reality, the choice was already made. Esther, his wife and queen, was far more important to him than Haman.

Haman knew this and tried to make the most of his final moments, by begging Esther for forgiveness (verses 7-8). However, instead of throwing himself on her mercy he ends up throwing himself on her couch... just as the king is returning from the garden. Whether it was because Haman had drunk too much or was simply overcome with emotion, the scene is another classic of world literature. It is almost like something from a farce. The king sees Haman bearing down on poor Esther... and it pushed his anger levels even higher: "Will this vile enemy Haman molest my dear wife Esther even while she is with me in my own house?!"

The end of verse 8 is so ominous. The king's attendants had been quickly mobilised while the king was in the garden and they were most efficient in dealing with the problem of this 'vile Haman'. As soon as the king spoke, they covered Haman's face (possibly with a blanket) in order to silence him and to symbolically indicate that he was no longer a person in the king's presence.

Finally, verse 9, one of the king's eunuch advisors had something useful to say. He seems to point out of the window at the 75 foot high 'tree' that Haman had erected in his back garden. Harbona explained that the structure had been built to murder Mordecai, *the man who had so recently been honoured for saving the life of the king*.

For once, the king was very decisive, needing none of his drinking buddies to suggest a course of action: hang Haman on the 'tree'! Haman dies the God-forsaken death, hanging on a tree, that he so justly deserved. He was a man truly under the curse of the Living God – because he had set himself as an enemy of the Bride of the Living God, the Church.

Just as Xerxes could not bear for Haman to molest his wife, so the Eternal Lord Jesus could not bear it either. Xerxes and the Lord Jesus agreed about one thing: Haman had to die a cursed death for molesting their brides, Esther and the Church.

The rise and fall of Haman is the biblical illustration for the theology of Psalm 73.

> "I envied the arrogant when I saw the prosperity of the wicked. They have no struggles; their bodies are healthy and strong. They are free from the burdens common to man; they are not plagued by human ills. Therefore pride is their necklace; they clothe themselves with violence. From their callous hearts comes iniquity; the evil conceits of their minds know no limits. They scoff, and speak with malice; in their arrogance they threaten oppression... When I tried to understand all this, it was oppressive to me *till I entered the sanctuary of God; then I understood their final destiny.*

Surely you place them on slippery ground; you cast them down to ruin. *How suddenly are they destroyed*, completely swept away by terrors! As a dream when one awakes, so when you arise, O Lord, you will despise them as fantasies." Psalm 73:3-8, 16-20

2. The Exaltation of Mordecai (8:1-2)

Early that same morning Mordecai was moments away from being sentenced to death on Haman's 'tree'... by the end of the day he had been lifted up for sure, but in a far better and more glorious way!

King Xerxes gave the estate of Haman to Esther, and Esther put Mordecai in charge of it. Mordecai was now granted direct access to the king, something that even Esther herself had been frightened of only a week before. The fact that Mordecai was related to Esther was good enough for Xerxes.

The signet ring of the king held fantastical power. When its mark was fixed to a decree, the law could never be changed or overturned. Yet, Xerxes was prepared to hand that ring over to Mordecai. Mordecai's elevation was so rapid he must have been quite dizzy!

The theme of the reversal of fortunes is so powerfully presented. That is what the Father, Son and Holy Spirit love to do. They love to turn the expectations and possibilities of the world upside down... often at the very moment that it seems least possible. The fact that the Trinity is so delighted by such 'last minute' reversals means that we should pray with great confidence and trust even in the very darkest and hardest times. When all human hope is gone, then we can still pray with hope and faith.

Even if we do not experience the kind of temporary glory that Mordecai experienced, we know that the exaltation we will enjoy when Jesus returns will be infinitely more than anything in the book of Esther. We will be really 'dizzy' on that great and glorious day when everything in the world is put the *right* way up!

3. Overturning Haman's edict (8:3-17)

The source of the problems had been dealt with, but the sentence of death still was hanging over the ancient Church.

The unbreakable edict of the king had already been issued. These laws could not be revoked. What could be done to enable the saints to survive?

Esther had to once again approach the king and once again the golden sceptre had to be offered to show her mercy. Xerxes seems a more sympathetic figure now that he is listening to Esther rather than Haman and his other 'advisors'.

Esther, with great care and diplomacy, appeals to the power of Xerxes. The laws cannot be repealed, but could another law be made that cancelled out the first? Xerxes reminds them that Haman's edict cannot be revoked, but he gives them full discretionary power to formulate a new edict that would nullify Haman's edict.

Once again the vast, international bureaucracy of the Persian empire swung into action. The royal secretaries were summoned to produce the edict, formulated by Mordecai. It was translated into all the relevant languages and posted out to all the 127 provinces of the vast empire. Mounted couriers on the very best horses raced to get the edict to every location as soon as possible.

It must have felt so strange for Esther and Mordecai. The power that was about to destroy them was now serving them.

So, what was the content of Mordecai's edict? How was he able to nullify Haman's plans? Well, he basically used Haman's edict as his template and changed the words so that those who attacked the saints were to be killed. Haman's excess of violent language is retained in this new edict: "to destroy, kill and annihilate any *armed* force..." However, notice that this capital punishment would not fall indiscriminately. Death would only come to "any armed force" that tried to carry out Haman's edict on the relevant day.

It had been an extraordinary time for Mordecai. He had been on the edge of a cursed, God-forsaken death and now was exalted to the highest place (8:15). He was clothed in the royal purple robes of honour and power, wearing a large crown of gold. The whole city celebrated with Mordecai and the Jews.

Verse 17 is one of my very favourite. The Jews throughout the whole empire enjoyed a time of great celebration and joy... and the outcome was that many other people wanted to become Jews as well.

"And many people of other nationalities became Jews because fear of the Jews had seized them."

People of every nation saw that there was a Living God in the heavens, a God more powerful than the deities and powers of Persia, more powerful than the powers of all creation.

The 127 provinces stretched from India to Egypt, covering all kinds of people and cultures, yet they could all see the gospel truth of the LORD God of Israel.

This moment of great deliverance resulted in the conversion of an international multitude, just as had happened at the time of the Exodus, in Exodus 12:38.

"Many other people went up with them, as well as large droves of livestock, both flocks and herds."

Israel has always been an international people destined to bless all the nations of the world. Today people from every tribe and nation, speaking all the languages of the world, form the global family of Israel.

The fact that Mordecai and the rest of the ancient Church were given such favour in the eyes of Xerxes was because of the intercession and mediation of Esther. For this reason, many commentators over the years see Esther as a Messianic figure.

The great Bible scholar, Henrietta Mears, subtitles her chapter on this book: "Esther portrays Jesus Christ, Our Advocate." Certainly, as we think about the overall story of Esther we can see how valuable it is to have an advocate with the powers on high. If this is true in earthly matters then how very much more in heavenly.

Both Haman and Esther were always under the control of the Living God. We are amazed at the way that the LORD God works His glorious will and purpose. Whether we trust Him as His saints or oppose Him as His enemies, we are all under His sovereign power.

Proverbs 16:4 "The LORD works out everything for his own ends – even the wicked for a day of disaster."

Study 5 Bible Questions

Esther 8:1-10

1. Verse 1-2. What a change for Esther and the ancient church! She had actually inherited the estate of Haman. Why did the Holy Spirit record this detail for us? See Matthew 5:5.
2. Verse 3-4. A famous Bible scholar of the 17th century compared the way that Esther approaches Xerxes and the way that we are received by God the Father. When we consider Hebrews 10:19-22, how does Xerxes compare to our Heavenly Father?
3. Verse 5. Why does Esther's 'prayer' begin with so many uses of the word "if"? What does this tell us about her relationship with Xerxes?
4. Verse 6. Esther is identified with the rest of the ancient church. Their fate is her fate. How should this apply to us today? How does the suffering of our Christian family affect us day to day?
5. Verses 7-8. It might seem strange that Xerxes doesn't make the decree himself. Can we think of any reasons why Xerxes hands this work over to Esther and Mordecai?
6. Esther 8:9 is the longest verse in the whole Bible... and it is a verses that stretches across the whole of Xerxes' mighty empire. In the light of all we thought about this great empire in chapter 1, why is this such an important verse?

Study 5 Further Questions

1. Xerxes was a difficult man to deal with. Such great power had corrupted him and filled him with high thoughts of himself. His use of the people around him and the way they had to speak to him all indicate the damage worldly power had done to him. How can a Christian deal with such power safely? How could a local church help someone in a position of great power?
2. How should we deal with those who are in positions of great power? What does the book of Proverbs tell us about 'handling' kings?
3. A law was such a great blessing to the ancient church. Mordecai's orders of Esther 8:9 saved the church from destruction. There are those who think that the way to bring about a righteous society is by working to enact 'righteous' laws. Others say that the answer lies only at the level of individuals being saved. What is the Biblical balance?

Study 5 Daily Readings

Day 1	Esther 7:1-10
Day 2	Esther 8:1-10
Day 3	Esther 8:11-17
Day 4	Psalm 9:1-20
Day 5	Proverbs 26:1-28
Day 6	Psalm 35:1-10
Day 7	Psalm 35:11-28

The daily Bible readings are an opportunity not only to read through all of the material in the book under study, but also to read parts of the Bible that relate to the themes and issues that we have been considering. We try to make sure that we receive light from the whole Bible as we think through the key issues each week.

Study 6 The Church under Divine Power

Esther chapters 9-10

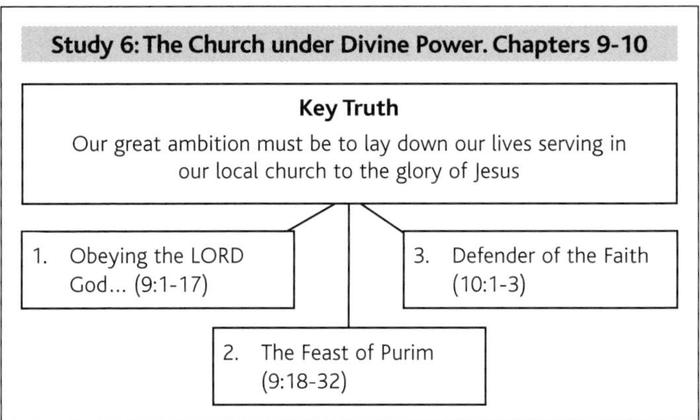

1. Obeying the LORD God... (9:1-17)

A film of the book of Esther might end with a glorious happy scene depicting the end of chapter 8, but the Bible has a more complicated ending in mind for us.

It is not enough for us to see the joyful celebrations of the saints and the new respect and power they have throughout the world. More than that we need to see that the verdict of the LORD God against the Amalekites, that was pronounced so very long ago, was carried out and pursued to the final limit.

Why do we need to see this? Why does the book of Esther want to display such a brutal conclusion to the story?

If we are comfortable people who live relatively comfortable lives then our 'enemies' are people who cut us up in traffic, take the credit for our work, throw their rubbish over the fence into our gardens, keep us awake at night with loud parties, are hard to get on with, make rude comments about us. In other words, our 'enemies' are not likely to confront us with

matters of life and death. Their actions cause inconvenience and upset to us, but the courts of heaven are hardly shaken by their behaviour towards us.

For many people in the world, their enemies are much more serious and their actions really do cause an outcry that is heard in the heavenly throne room. Those that suffer serious abuse and injustice call out to the Living God as the only one who can give them help or hope. They are killed, raped, enslaved and humiliated... yet there seems to be no possibility of overthrowing the tyrant. These enemies of humanity are enemies of the LORD God, who defends the widow and the orphan.

When the Amalekites killed the weak and wounded of the Hebrews in the exodus from Egypt, they showed a terrible heartlessness and cruelty. They showed how godless they were by this viscous slaughter. The problem of the human condition is so not always so clearly seen. If we live far from the Living God then the darkness gets ever deeper into our souls and we are driven further away from light and love and goodness.

The LORD God saw the hardness and evil in the Amalekite people. Their wicked lives provoked His anger and His verdict was just and true. There was time for repentance, but the Amalekites remained entrenched in their godlessness and cruelty. In the case of the people of Jericho, although they were all under the fatal judgment of the LORD, yet Rahab found mercy as she joined with the Hebrews.[26] In the case of the Amalekites, they seemed to have harboured their evil and malice down the generations. Finally, under the leadership of Saul the day of judgement arrived and they were mostly removed from the LORD's earth.

However, as we saw, Saul's disobedience left a root to re-grow.

When we get to the book of Esther and hear that the Amalekites have not only escaped the LORD's judgement but have spread and spun new threats, if we have taken on the heart and mind of the LORD Jesus, we are crying out for justice against them. It is a major insult to the LORD's glory that they have been allowed to thrive whilst spitting in His face.

When we have a heart that is moved to compassion and practical love like Jesus but also a heart that rejoices when Jesus delivers His perfect justice, then we have a heart that is truly divine. It is all too easy for us to have a hard heart that looks only for judgement or a soft head that

26 Joshua 6

cannot understand justice. We need to walk in step with the Spirit till we have a heart full of compassion and justice, love and truth.

Verses 16-17 show us what happened throughout the world on that day of judgement.

> Meanwhile, the remainder of the Jews who were in the king's provinces also assembled to protect themselves and get relief from their enemies. They killed seventy-five thousand of them but did not lay their hands on the plunder. This happened on the thirteenth day of the month of Adar, and on the fourteenth they rested and made it a day of feasting and joy.

There will be a day when we will join with the LORD Jesus in His great glory as we judge the world, even passing judgement on the angels. Speaking personally, though I long for justice, I find it hard to imagine being capable of such clear and wise justice. Nevertheless, the Old Testament (as we have it in our English Bibles), ends with an incredible vision where the church joins the LORD Jesus in destroying the wicked on the final day of judgement. Malachi 4:1-3

> Surely the day is coming; it will burn like a furnace. All the arrogant and every evildoer will be stubble, and that day that is coming will set them on fire," says the LORD Almighty. "Not a root or a branch will be left to them. But for you who revere my name, the sun of righteousness will rise with healing in its wings. And you will go out and leap like calves released from the stall. Then you will trample down the wicked; they will be ashes under the soles of your feet on the day when I do these things," says the LORD Almighty.

2. The Feast of Purim. (9:18-32)

Through Moses, the LORD Jesus established all kinds of wonderful festivals to punctuate the year. The key theological truths that reveal reality were written into the calendar so that throughout the year the saints were led into all kinds of experiences of gospel truth as they waited for the Promised Messiah. Whether celebrating the way the blood of the lamb caused the judgement to pass over them when they were redeemed from Egypt or the way they lived in tents for a week to remind them that we are only pilgrims and refugees on our way to our true home of the future. These feasts were given by the LORD to help His ancient church keep the reality of Jesus the Messiah in their hearts and minds while they waited for Him to be born.

The fascinating occurrence at the end of Esther 9 is that the ancient church decided to make a new feast dedicated to the celebration of the fact that the Living God governs every detail of reality for the good of those that love Him. The specific events of the book of Esther would be recalled every year to keep this glorious truth at the heart of the church.

Some Christians struggle with the idea of any Christian festivals at all. Some are worried that our Christian ancestors colonised *pagan* festivals with the birth, life, death, and resurrection of Jesus. In order to drown out the winter solstice or the spring pagan festivals, the Christians tried to take over these feast times with a much better celebration based on spiritual reality rather than spiritual darkness.

Not all Christians are persuaded that this was the best thing to do. Some fear that pagan elements have infiltrated into the Christian celebrations.

Speaking for my own family, we appreciate these festivals as opportunities not only to explore specific aspects of Jesus person and work, but also opportunities to introduce outsiders to these realities. Very few people know anything about the pagan festivals that were taken over by the Jesus-festivals. In many ways this very fact is a testimony to the success of these Christian festivals introduced by our ancestors.

3. Defender of the Faith (10:1-3)

The book of Esther ends with such a curiously short chapter. It is difficult to understand what the 13th century church leaders had in mind when they divided up Esther in this way![27]

> King Xerxes imposed tribute throughout the empire, to its distant shores. And all his acts of power and might, together with a full account of the greatness of Mordecai to which the king had raised him, are they not written in the book of the annals of the kings of Media and Persia? Mordecai the Jew was second in rank to King Xerxes, preeminent among the Jews, and held in high esteem by his many fellow Jews, because he worked for the good of his people and spoke up for the welfare of all the Jews.

27 Archbishop of Canterbury Stephen Langton and Cardinal Hugo de Sancto Caro developed the chapter and verse divisions in the first half of the 13th century AD.

The book of Esther tells us that if we want to know more about King Xerxes the official histories of the Persian kings is the place to look. That in itself is an interesting point. Archaeologists or standard historians might well imagine that the most important information for the period would be all about Xerxes and his armies and empire. They might want to study how the Xerxes that we meet in Esther comes up against the Spartan armies in the following years. They might want to study the rise and fall of these mighty human empires. However, the book of Esther tells us to look elsewhere if that is what is on our agenda. The key to understanding the book of Esther is not detailed background information about Xerxes or the Persian empire. The book of Esther is revealing deep truths to us about the church of the Living God and the wonderful, mysterious, omnipotent, jealous love that the LORD God has for His Bride.

The book of Esther holds up Mordecai rather than Esther for our admiration and consideration. Mordecai worked for the good of the church and for this he is honoured. If we too lay down our lives for the mission and good of the church then we too will invest in eternal treasure. The church is Jesus answer to the problems of the world. It is the community where people can find help and comfort, where people will plead the cause of the widow and the orphan, the place where we sell what we have in order to help those in need, where forgiveness, challenge, truth and love can be found.

Bill Hybels of Willow Creek church wrote a tremendous statement about the local church. We project it up onto the screen at the beginning of our Sunday morning meetings and it has inspired me to follow the example of Mordecai.

> There is nothing like the local church when it's working right. Its beauty is indescribable. Its power is breathtaking. Its potential is unlimited. It comforts the grieving and heals the broken in the context of community. It builds bridges to seekers and offers truth to the confused. It provides resources for those in need and opens its arms to the forgotten, the downtrodden, the disillusioned. It breaks the chains of addictions, frees the oppressed, and offers belonging to the marginalized of this world.

Study 6 Bible Questions

Esther 9:20-32

1. Verse 20-21. If Mordecai had sent orders of judgment in Esther 8:9, now he sends orders of celebration. Given the glorious events recorded in the last sentence of Esther chapter 8, would it have been enough to write these letters in Hebrew alone?
2. Verse 22a. What was the theme of the festival of Purim? What were all these new Jews from all the other nations actually celebrating?
3. Verse 22b. How was Purim celebrated? What were the key ingredients in the festival? Why was this a good way to celebrate what had happened?
4. Verse 23-25. Mordecai suggested this festival to the ancient church. In the summary of the book in these verses, why isn't Esther even mentioned?
5. Verses 26-27. How could the Jews take 'it on themselves to establish the custom' of Purim?
6. Verse 28. Why was it so important that all Jews everywhere celebrated this festival?
7. Verses 29-32. Why is Esther mentioned so much in these verses?
8. Do you think it is good for Christians to all unite together to celebrate the different aspects of what Jesus has done for us?

Study 6 Further Questions

1. What do you think of the traditional Christian festivals? Would they be better if they were at different times of the year away from any ancient pagan festivals? Is it possible to capture 'pagan' festivities and 'baptise' them for Jesus? Would Christmas be better if it was only celebrated by genuine Jesus-followers?
2. In Esther 9:19 & 22 we see how giving presents to each other was a key part of Purim. Could this be a good Biblical defense of Christmas presents?
3. Could we establish new festivals today? If some great events happened to the modern church, should we institute a new festival? What events might be worth such a big celebration?

Study 6 Daily Readings

Day 1	Esther 9:1-19
Day 2	Esther 9:20-32
Day 3	Esther 10:1-3
Day 4	Exodus 14:1-31
Day 5	Exodus 15:1-21
Day 6	2 Samuel 22:1-25
Day 7	2 Samuel 22:26-51

The daily Bible readings are an opportunity not only to read through all of the material in the book under study, but also to read parts of the Bible that relate to the themes and issues that we have been considering. We try to make sure that we receive light from the whole Bible as we think through the key issues each week.

Suggested Answers to the Bible Study Questions

Study 1 Bible Answers

Esther 1:1-12

1. Christians lived under the Roman Empire. In more recent times Christians lived under the Nazis and still live under Communism. The church can feel so small and powerless under such mighty empires.
2. Xerxes was the great global power. He was the king who was bringing the whole world under his one great kingdom.
3. People had to travel so far to get to see his treasure and possessions. It would take weeks and weeks to travel from the edges to the centre. He also would want everybody to have a chance to see how great he was.
4. It is as if Xerxes models himself on the Living God. His palace is an earthly echo of the city of God.
5. Each region would have had different vineyards with all kinds of different grapes. The fact that he could offer the best wine from every region was an amazing statement to the reach and wealth of his kingdom. His city and palace would seem to be unbelievably sophisticated to the provincial visitors.
6. Xerxes has no room for any other glory or majesty in his world. His wife is treated as a mere footnote. Women were not treated as equal partners in the gracious gift of life.
7. He makes big decisions when he is drunk. He chooses bad advisors. The rest of Proverbs 31 reveals a much better understanding of wives than Xerxes could ever know.
8. Materialism, capitalism, Islam and communism are all mighty empires. It is vital for us to remember who really controls the world. We need to pray as to the Great King who can grant all things.

Study 2 Bible Answers

Section reference

1. The women were treated as objects rather than people. Things are done to them rather than by them. They are passive rather than active. Women are seen as possessions.
2. Daniel was in a position of more personal independence, yet both were forced into a pattern of life in slavery. Their diet was controlled for them. They were 'managed'.
3. When we consider the whole book of Esther we can see this was the right thing to do. There are many Muslims today who believe in Jesus but are not yet able to be very public about this. We should pray for them and offer any support we can. It is not for us to put pressure on such people if we don't face those dangers.
4. The key seems to be understanding where our true beauty lies. If it starts to depend on the external treatments, then we may need to think again.
5. Xerxes had a whole system set up to please his every desire, his every whim.
6. Esther had a good reputation, with the full confidence of Hegai. She won the admiration of everybody. She had a good character, showing that her beauty came from deeper than mere beauty treatments.
7. Esther had lost her family and was isolated away from the church family. She was forced to conform to an alien culture and work in an environment of selfishness and pride. Yet, she retained her character. She knew that the Living God was in control. However, it must have been a very difficult and confusing time.

Study 3 Bible Answers

Esther 3:1-11

1. The Agagites were the distant descendants of the Amalekites who had mercilessly murdered the Israelites during the Exodus. Putting Haman in power would have been terrifying to the ancient church. Haman's ancestors had brutally killed them. The plans of the Living God usually run deeper and wider than we can see at the time.
2. Mordecai could not go along with the worship of Haman without dishonouring the Living God. The LORD God had commanded that all the Amalekites should be destroyed. Mordecai had reached one of those crucial moments when we have to draw a line and stand by it.
3. When we face a collision between human laws and the LORD Jesus, then we must always follow Jesus. We should not look for such challenges, but if they come we must not be cowards.
4. Haman understands the ancient history at stake here just as well as Mordecai does. Haman would like to finish the job that his ancestors began.
5. The lot was cast in the first month, yet the date set was in the last month. This meant that they had the maximum amount of time to get ready.
6. The ancient church maintained a distinct lifestyle even among all the different cultures of Xerxes' empire. Just as we do, they would have faced all kinds of choices about how to respond to all the different aspects of life in the world. However, they were seen as living differently.
7. Haman seems to be out of control, but in reality, as we shall see, he was just as much under the LORD's control as the casting of the lot.

Study 4 Bible Answers

Esther 4:1-14

1. Sackcloth and ashes symbolizes repentance and sorrow. Wearing these things usually goes along with prayer and humility. See Daniel 9:3.
2. King Xerxes did not want signs of repentance or mourning in his presence. He wanted feasts and celebrations, but not signs that there were deep problems to face.
3. There was a great unity across the world within the church. They all understood the seriousness of the situation. Nothing tends to remind the church of its unity and its need for prayer as persecution.
4. Esther seems to have been isolated in the palace from the normal events of public life.
5. Mordecai tells Hathak the amount of money to be used in destroying the church; a copy of the edict and instructions for Esther to plead for mercy for the church. Esther had to be brought right up to speed on the desperate nature of the situation.
6. Xerxes court was a place of fear. Esther might die just for trying to speak to Xerxes.
7. If Esther was cut off from the normal issues of imperial life, she needed to know that she could not escape what was happening outside the palace.
8. The Living God would deliver them one way or another. His Church cannot be destroyed. The Living God could manage with or without Esther – but she could not manage if she turned from the LORD God.
9. The whole book of Esther shows us how the apparent madness and chaos of sinful human power is actually under the ultimate sovereign power of the Father, Son and Holy Spirit.

Study 5 Bible Answers

Esther 8:1-10

1. However impossible it might seem, the meek followers of Jesus will ultimately inherit everything in the world.
2. We can approach with confidence and safety into the Father's presence. We are commanded to come right up to His throne to tell Him all that makes us anxious. Xerxes does not make anyone feel welcome or secure in his presence, not even his own wife.
3. Esther is so uncertain of Xerxes' favour that she has to be so very cautious about asking him for anything.
4. Esther cannot bear for the church to suffer. Can we bear the fact that our brothers and sisters are being harmed? How does this disturb us? What do we do about it?
5. Xerxes tends to delegate important matters to others and he does not understand the ways or character of the ancient church. He has not taken the cause of the church into himself. He merely *allows* them to protect themselves. Unlike Jesus, who takes the safety of the church into Himself, taking their suffering onto Himself. Think of Acts 9:4.
6. The global empire might have seemed such a threatening place, yet the power of this human empire could be turned to serve the kingdom of God.

Study 6 Bible Answers

Esther 9:20-32

1. If many people of other nationalities had become Jews, then it may have got much more complicated for Mordecai to send letters out to all the Jews in the empire. Now he may have had to translate it into far more languages – like had happened in 1:22.
2. It was a celebration of the fact that the Jews got relief from their enemies. The multinational Jewish community could celebrate the fact that the Living God had defended His Bride, and always would do.
3. The four components of the festival were feasting; joy; giving food presents to each other and giving gifts to poor people. It seems likely that the gifts to the poor went beyond the church community, reaching out to needy people in the empire.
4. Esther's role in the destruction of Haman was a private matter of court life. The decrees that Mordecai wrote were a matter of public knowledge.
5. The LORD God is never mentioned in this book. Even if He had sent a prophet or a dream or vision to command this, it would not be explicitly recorded in this book. However, it seems that the LORD is happy for us to think up occasions for praising all that He has done for us!
6. The danger had been against the entire ancient church, so it was important for the entire church to celebrate their deliverance together.
7. It was important to show that this letter came with the full authority of the royal household. This letter was also a matter of public record.
8. Christmas, Easter and Ascension day are commonly celebrated across the world.